Communication in Times of Trouble

Communication in Times of Trouble

Best Practices for Crisis and Emergency Risk
Communication

Matthew W. Seeger

Timothy L. Sellnow

WILEY Blackwell

This edition first published 2019
© 2019 John Wiley & Sons, Inc.

The right of Matthew W. Seeger and Timothy L. Sellnow to be identified as the author(s)
of this work has been asserted in accordance with law.

Registered Office
John Wiley & Sons, Inc., 111 River Street, Hoboken, NJ 07030, USA

Editorial Office
101 Station Landing, Medford, MA 02155, USA

For details of our global editorial offices, customer services, and more information about
Wiley products visit us at www.wiley.com.

Wiley also publishes its books in a variety of electronic formats and by print-on-demand.
Some content that appears in standard print versions of this book may not be available in
other formats.

Library of Congress Cataloging-in-Publication Data

Names: Seeger, Matthew W. (Matthew Wayne), 1957– author. |
   Sellnow, Timothy L. (Timothy Lester), 1960– author.
Title: Communication in times of trouble : best practices for crisis and emergency
   risk communication / Matthew W. Seeger, Timothy L. Sellnow.
Description: 1st edition. | Hoboken, NJ : Wiley-Blackwell, [2019] |
   Includes bibliographical references and index. |
Identifiers: LCCN 2018052533 (print) | LCCN 2019001384 (ebook) |
   ISBN 9781119229261 (Adobe PDF) | ISBN 9781119235019 (ePub) |
   ISBN 9781119229247 (hardcover) | ISBN 9781119229254 (paperback)
Subjects: LCSH: Communication in crisis management.
Classification: LCC HD49.3 (ebook) | LCC HD49.3 .S435 2019 (print) |
   DDC 658.4/5–dc23
LC record available at https://lccn.loc.gov/2018052533

Cover Design: Wiley
Cover Image: Courtesy of Joan Ferguson

Set in 10/12pt Warnock by SPi Global, Pondicherry, India

Printed in Singapore by C.O.S. Printers Pte Ltd

10   9   8   7   6   5   4   3   2   1

Contents

Acknowledgements

The field of crisis and emergency communication continues to grow. Crises and disasters are occurring more frequently, commanding more attention and generating more research. Chief executive officers and managers are increasingly realizing that effectively preparing for and responding to a crisis require effective communication. The resulting expansion in research and theory regarding crisis communication has created the need for synthesis and summary.

"Best Practices in Crisis Communication: An Expert Panel Process" was published in 2006 in the *Journal of Applied Communication Research*. The essay had the goal of providing a set of accessible guidelines for crisis planning and response. Although there has been some debate about the individual formulation of these 10 best practices, they have generally held up for more than a decade. This book expands on that essay and presents these 10 best practices as a set of accessible principles that can help inform both research and practice.

There are many people to thank for their patience and support including our spouses, Beth and Deanna, and our children, Maggie and Henry and Debbie and Rick. We also would like to especially thank Ashleigh Day, Stephanie Church, and Sydney Wallace for research and editorial support.

Many colleagues and current and former students allow us to share ideas: Laura Pechta, Marsha Vanderford, Barbara Reynolds, Keri Lubell, Charles Bantz, Joel Iverson, Dennis Gouran, Lee Wilkins, Bill Benoit, Tim Coombs, Andreas Swartz, Dan O'Hair, Kevin Barge, Robert Littlefield, Robert Heath, Finn Frandsen, Keith Hearit, Robert Rowland, Ron Arnett, Jeanne Persuit, Donyale Padgett, Julie Novak, Brooke Liu, Yan Jin, Amiso George, Hamilton Bean, Shawn McElmurry, Steven Venette, Patric Spence, Ken Lachlan, Adam Parrish, Jeff Brand, Robert Ulmer, Melvin Gupton, Colleen Ezzeddine, Catherine Galentine, Suzanne Horsley and Christine Yi-Hui Huang, J. J. McIntyre, Alyssa Millner, Elizabeth Petrun Sayers, Kathryn Anthony, Bethney Wilson, Morgan Getchell, Emina

Herovic, Emily Helsel, Maxwell Kuchenreuther, Rebecca Freihaut, Julie Smith, Nathan Stewart, and many others.

We hope this work is useful to the next generation of crisis scholars and practitioners who will likely find themselves needing to communicate in times of trouble.

We dedicate this work to Seneca Jane Swift and Lincoln Robert Sellnow-Richmond.

1

Introduction

Our world is increasingly complex. Companies and organizations are larger than ever and are tightly connected by complex and changing technologies and long supply chains. Daunting and complicated issues like climate change, population shifts and migration, and global political instability create very rapid and widespread change. Many critical resources such as water and energy are in increasingly short supply. Social, political, environmental, and economic conditions seem unstable and unpredictable. Ways of operating, doing business, making a living, interacting with others, and communicating are constantly evolving. The high level of complexity and change is matched by an escalating number and severity of emergencies, disasters, and crises.

Bad things are happening all the time, all around us. It seems like social media and old or legacy media are constantly reporting on a new threat, crisis, or disaster. Severe weather (e.g., hurricanes, tornadoes, blizzards, floods, heat waves, and droughts) occurs throughout the United States and around the world. Most climate scientists predict more extreme weather because of global climate change. Spills of toxic materials (e.g., oil, industrial chemicals, sewage, and even radiological material) are increasingly common. Earthquakes are regular events in some parts of the world and are among the deadliest naturally occurring crises. In addition, they can lead to secondary crises, such as tsunamis, toxic spills, and industrial disasters, as was the case with the Fukushima Daiichi nuclear disaster in Japan in 2011. Mass shooting and workplace violence, sadly, appear to be happening more often. The 2012 shooting at Sandy Hook Elementary School in Newtown, Conn., killed 20 children and 6 adult staff members. The Parkland, Fla., shootings claimed 17 lives. Transportation accidents, terrorist events, defective products, plant explosions, criminal activity, infectious diseases, and sudden economic downturns all can be considered crises (Sellnow & Seeger, 2013).

Communication in Times of Trouble: Best Practices for Crisis and Emergency Risk Communication, First Edition. Matthew W. Seeger and Timothy L. Sellnow.
© 2019 John Wiley & Sons, Inc. Published 2019 by John Wiley & Sons, Inc.

Because our society is more complex, technologically sophisticated, dynamic, and interdependent than ever before, these crises can be very disruptive and destructive. Contamination of a basic food product, such as peanut paste, may have consequences for hundreds of consumer products, including cookies, crackers, cakes, cereals, candy, and other snack foods. The 2008 *Salmonella* contamination at Peanut Corporation of America led to the recall of almost 4,000 separate products that contained the company's peanut paste. A relatively small defect in a safety device may end up in thousands of cars, prompting industry-wide recalls. Takata Corporation's defective airbags were installed in dozens of automotive models. At least 12 companies and over 19 million cars were involved in the recall that likely cost the company at least $5 billion. An outbreak of an infectious disease in a remote part of the world can slow and limit air travel, cost billions in medical preparation, and create global fear. The 2014 Ebola outbreak in West Africa dominated media coverage for weeks and became a significant political issue in the United States because of fears the disease could jump to other parts of the world.

The ways we prepare for, respond to, and understand these and other crisis events are influenced by our communication. Risk communication, the process of informing people about potential hazards, is a central activity in helping people prepare for a crisis. The U.S. Department of Homeland Security (DHS) for example, has created a Ready.Gov website and a series of "Preparing Makes Sense" public service announcements to communicate risk information (U.S. Department of Homeland Security, 2015). Crisis communication is essential to emergency management. Alerts such as tornado warnings or fire alarms signal that we need to take immediate action in response to a risk. A tornado warning means there is an immediate risk of severe weather and people should take cover. A fire alarm signals a fire has been detected and people should leave the building. Communication helps us learn about risks and how to avoid them. Communication gives us information so we understand what to do in a crisis. After a crisis is over, communication is the process that helps us determine who to blame for what happened, what we can learn, and how to move beyond the destruction and loss.

What Is a Crisis?

Think for a moment about a traumatic event you experienced. Perhaps it involved severe weather, a fire, a transportation accident, or a flood. Maybe it's something a family member went through or an event you watched develop through the media. What were the event's primary features that made you think of this as a crisis? How did you feel? Were you confused and afraid? What did you do? Did you seek out information and ask others for help? Were you instructed to take some specific action, such as seek shelter or evacuate? What harms occurred as a consequence of the crisis?

We perceive an event as a crisis based on several characteristics and not everyone will see the same event as a crisis. In some regions, a major snowstorm is a routine event and would not be seen as a crisis. In fact, the lack of snow in these regions might be seen as a disruptive and threatening development because people depend on winter tourism. Contamination of a municipal water supply and a boil water advisory might be seen as an annoyance for the first few hours or even the first day, but it will soon develop into a crisis.

Typically, a crisis is seen as a threatening event. Some high-priority goals, such as personal safety, health, or financial stability, are at risk. Sometimes the threat is to the safety of family, friends, pets, property, or community. In other cases, the threat is to reputation, career, or job or economic security. Almost always there is a feeling and a fear that something you value, something very important to you, might be harmed or lost. This threat to something that is highly valued is one of the defining characteristics of a crisis.

A crisis is also associated with uncertainty. Uncertainty is related to an inability to predict an outcome, anticipate what will happen next, or simply to deal with how little is known about what is happening and what might happen. Usually a crisis is not expected and is very surprising and shocking. For example, earthquakes typically occur with very little warning, even though there is good information about where earthquakes happen most frequently. Transportation accidents, fires, and terrorist events are also usually surprising. In other cases, crises are more predictable and less surprising. Hurricanes and tornadoes tend to occur in somewhat predictable locations at the same time of year and, although they may be surprising, are not unexpected. Some crises, such as infectious disease outbreaks or environmental contaminations, are slow moving and may last for months or even years. Predicting their onset is possible even if avoiding them is not. The annual influenza (flu) season regularly claims several thousand lives and typically does not escalate to the level of a serious epidemic. Even in cases where a crisis is predictable, there is still a great deal of uncertainty about what will happen as a consequence of the crisis.

One way a crisis creates uncertainty is by disrupting our sense of what is normal. The flu season is a normal, regular event and most of us know specific steps, such as getting a flu shot, washing hands, and covering coughs and sneezes, can limit the risk of getting sick. In some cases, flu can become a very serious threat to public health, such as the 1918 so-called Spanish flu, which killed between 50 and 100 million people worldwide (Taubenberger & Morens, 2006). When a crisis disrupts our sense of what is normal, we no longer have a clear sense of what to do, how to avoid risks, and what will happen next. In some recent cases of serious flu outbreaks, large public events were reduced or canceled to reduce the spread of the disease.

A final aspect of crisis many people experience is the need to take some action to reduce uncertainty or to contain and offset the harm. This may involve collecting information about what is happening, evacuating neighborhoods, boiling water, or helping victims. Generally, these actions must happen quickly to limit the harm. During tornadoes, for example, public warnings tell people to take cover immediately to save lives. When water supplies are contaminated with bacteria, the more quickly people stop drinking or treat the water through actions such as boiling, the lower the risk that large numbers of people will get sick. Any delay in issuing a boil water advisory can increase the level of harm.

Perceived threat, high levels of uncertainty, and short response time are three defining characteristics of most crises we experience. You probably observed all three conditions in the crisis you experienced and recognized the circumstances were not normal. Most, but not all, crises have all three elements; however, in general, a crisis is an event or series of events that are threatening, create high levels of uncertainty, and require some immediate response (Sellnow & Seeger, 2013). Crises are also disruptive to our sense of security and normalcy; generate high levels of confusion and uncertainty; result in anxiety, fear, and apprehension; and create a need to communicate. Communication is necessary to manage this crisis, reduce uncertainty, and limit the harm.

What Do We Mean by Crisis Communication?

Crisis communication is the process of planning, developing, and disseminating informational and persuasive messages for avoiding, containing, and managing harm from risky, threatening, and uncertain conditions. Crisis communication has many of the same features of other forms of communication, including senders, receivers, messages, and channels. Senders include the government agencies that oversee emergency responses or the organizations and agencies that have caused a crisis. During a crisis, senders are also those who are affected by the crisis or the media organizations reporting on the crisis. In most major crises, there are many senders and this sometimes creates confusing and conflicting messages.

We view receivers from an inclusive perspective. Rather than using terms such as the public or general public, we refer to receivers as publics. We choose this plural term because of the tremendous diversity of relevant audiences and their varying needs, values, backgrounds, and perspectives. Publics are communities and stakeholders with direct or indirect connections to an organization, an issue, or an event (Leitch & Motion, 2010). In a crisis, publics may include employees, customers, suppliers, neighbors, government, response agencies, media, and family members, as well as those individuals or groups directly affected by the event. Each of these groups may include members from diverse cultures, backgrounds, ethnicities, ages, income levels, and education. Considerable research in crisis and emergency communication shows that a failure to account for the cultural, ethnic, and social diversity of receivers as separate publics, for example, leads to failures in communication (Littlefield, 2013). Sensitivity to diversity is essential in the application of each of the best practices we describe in this book. In fact, some agencies, such as the Centers for Disease Control and Prevention (CDC) disseminate messages in many languages to ensure diverse communities have access to critical information during a crisis.

As with other forms of communication, crisis messages are disseminated through channels. Channels are what carry the message. During a crisis, one of the most important factors is how quickly a specific channel can get the message out to as many people as possible. Some new media channels, such as Twitter and Facebook, can be very fast, so much so that crisis agencies sometimes monitor social media to determine when a crisis happens. Traditional broadcast media, such as television and radio, also cover events in real time and can be very effective forms of crisis communication. Radio, because it is very resilient and widely available, is often used as a standard channel for crisis messages. Warning signals, such as fire alarms or tornado sirens, have been used for many years as ways to immediately get the attention of people and alert them of a risk. A second important feature of a crisis communication channel is how widely it distributes the message. Crisis messages must reach as many of the people who are at risk as possible. There are many cases of people who did not receive an evacuation warning because of how the message was distributed. Sometimes, crises occur at night when people are sleeping and they do not receive the message. Although Twitter and Facebook are very fast, some publics do not monitor these channels and would not receive a message distributed through these channels. Many people no longer watch television news and even fewer read traditional newspapers. In fact, only about 20% of people read a daily newspaper. Regardless of the channel used to initially disseminate a crisis message, most people will use direct face-to-face or person-to-person communication to confirm the risk or warn others. This may involve phone calls, text messages, or a quick check-in with neighbors and friends to see what they are doing during a crisis. In fact, many of us will first learn about a major crisis from another person, a friend or family member, before we turn to established mass media channels of communication for more information.

The development of social media channels has changed many of the ways we communicate during a crisis. Handheld mobile devices, such as cell phones and tablets, have allowed those experiencing a crisis to both send and receive information in real time. Pictures of floods or fires are often posted on Facebook pages and texted to friends and family members before journalists arrive on the scene. Response agencies can use social media to quickly update publics on developments, recommend actions, or address rumors through Twitter feeds or social media sites. Google maps have proved very useful in facilitating evacuations in cases of wildfires and floods. Text alerts are very important in alerting people to shelter in place during active shooter threats. Social media is very flexible and interactive, allowing for people experiencing a crisis and those managing it to exchange information in real time. In fact, social media can be used in implementing all of the best practices described in this book and should be included in any effort to manage a risk or crisis.

A final important feature of crisis communication channels concerns resilience. Some forms of communication are easily disrupted and take a very long time to repair. Traditional broadcast television, for example, can be very vulnerable to severe weather events. Cellular telephone networks can be disrupted by earthquakes, fires, or even attacks. Traditional newspapers often have both their production and delivery disrupted by a crisis. Radio, as we described earlier, is a very resilient form of communication and, in many cases, local radio stations disrupted by crises are quickly back on the air providing important information to the public. Most people have radios in their cars and many emergency management agencies recommend buying portable radios with built-in, hand-cranked generators. Radio can also be flexible and address the elements of a crisis as they emerge.

Communication can also help promote broader community resilience during a crisis. Community resilience is the ability of a community to utilize resources to avoid, respond to, withstand, and recover from adverse situations, such as crises. Resilience has many components, including the amount of connectedness, the availability of resources, the level of planning and preparation, and the level of vulnerability a community faces. Communication can promote connections between the elements that make up a community and help deploy and utilize resources effectively. Planning and preparedness as well as understanding risk requires communication. The Federal Emergency Management Agency (FEMA) developed a framework for crisis management called the Whole Community approach. This approach emphasizes government is just one component and the community itself must be empowered to prepare and respond if a crisis is to be managed successfully. This includes local community groups, companies, and schools. Through dialog, community assets can be organized and strengthened and responses can be more effective and efficient (FEMA, 2016).

What Distinguishes Crisis Communication?

A crisis is an extreme event that is abnormal, threatening, creates uncertainty, and requires a response. Crisis communication is the process of sending and receiving messages between senders and receivers about the risk of a crisis under the extreme conditions of a crisis. Communication is important to all stages of a crisis—before an event occurs, during the crisis, and after the crisis has ended. Before a crisis, communication helps publics understand risks, prepare and plan for risks, and avoid them when possible. During a crisis, communication is critical to coordinating response efforts, limiting harm, and deploying resources. After a crisis has subsided, communication helps us sort out blame and responsibility as well as learn and pass on the lessons from the crisis.

Communication professionals, public relations practitioners, public information officers, community liaisons, health communicators, journalists, social and digital media practitioners, technical writers, and webmasters are increasingly participating in risk communication. Effective communication is one of the most important resources necessary to manage risks and crisis. There are many cases where effective communication helped reduce a risk so a crisis never occurred and where communication helped limit the harm of a crisis. In fact, the vast majority of risks never become full crises. There are also many cases where failed communication made a crisis much worse and increased the harm to people, organizations, and communities.

What Are Best Practices?

In describing effective crisis communication, we present best practices as ways to improve practice (Seeger, 2006). A best practices approach is a way to describe techniques, methods, or guidelines that have been effective in most cases. A best practice is an industry standard or a widely accepted approach shown to lead to positive outcomes. These methods have typically been widely accepted and represent a recommended course of action. As new research and techniques develop, best practices can change and evolve. Developing and using best practices has been widely applied in business, medicine, education, engineering, government, and many other professional contexts. The goal of best practice research is to use the experiences of the past to develop practical knowledge and apply the lessons to improve operations (Steelman & McCaffrey, 2013; Veil & Husted, 2012).

A crisis is a complex and dynamic event, and each crisis is in some ways unique. Although best practices will not be successful in all cases, as general guidelines, they help us prepare and respond appropriately. A crisis creates a great deal of uncertainty, confusion, and chaos and most people have very limited experience responding to these events. Sometimes, crisis results in a kind of analysis paralysis where managers and communication professionals simply do not know what to do or say and, as a consequence, seem unable to respond. Under these conditions of high uncertainty and confusion about what to do, having basic guidelines about how to respond can be very helpful.

A best practices approach can help provide general guidance for crisis communication during the extreme conditions of a crisis. Because a crisis is an abnormal event creating high uncertainty, best practices can be especially helpful in guiding planning and response. The following sections in this book present 10 best practices for crisis communication. These are:

1) Take a process approach: A process approach to crisis communication emphasizes the connections between activities and outcomes and provides an outline of how a crisis evolves over time.

2) Engage in preevent planning: Planning crisis communication before an event occurs is very important in creating an effective response. Crisis communication plans are most effective when they are integrated with other plans and are connected to core values.

3) Form stakeholder partnerships with publics: Creating authentic dialogs and partnerships with diverse publics enhances cooperation. Strong partnerships with publics can create a reservoir of goodwill that can be critical during a crisis.

4) Listen to and acknowledge concerns of publics: Audience analysis is one of the key methods for improving communication. Listening to and acknowledging the concerns of publics allows messages to be adapted as a crisis evolves.

5) Communicate with honesty, frankness, and openness: Although it is often difficult to be honest, frank, and open during a crisis, these approaches are necessary to improve trust. Responding to a crisis with a public relations spin, withholding information, or refusing to comment is a very risky approach.

6) Collaborate and coordinate with credible sources: Many groups will be involved in a crisis response and collaboration and coordination with credible sources allows for more effective use of resources.
7) Meet the needs of the media: Media will report on most major crises and effective crisis communication must make use of both old and new media to disseminate messages. Providing access to the media can reduce confusion and rumors.
8) Communicate with compassion: Sometimes organizations are reluctant to express concern for fear of admitting responsibility. However, compassion in the form of concern and empathy is an important response whenever people have been harmed from a crisis.
9) Accept uncertainty and ambiguity: Uncertainty and ambiguity are always part of a crisis and being able to communicate under these conditions is critical to success. Not having all the answers does not mean there is no need to communicate.
10) Communicate messages of empowerment: Crisis can strip away our sense of personal control and messages that empower publics can help reduce stress and trauma. People have a basic need to do something in response to a crisis and it is important to provide some direction.

Summary

Crises are threatening and uncertain events that occur frequently. They have the potential to create very severe impacts and can profoundly damage communities, businesses, organizations, families, and individuals. One way to manage the risk and uncertainty of a crisis is through effective communication. In fact, communication is one of the most important tools for effective crisis management. It simply isn't possible to manage a crisis without communication. One method for improving crisis communication is using best practices. In the following chapters we describe how 10 best practices of crisis communication can improve effectiveness.

Key Takeaways for Communicating During Crisis

Crises occur often and are part of social, community, and organization life. Our complex, dynamic, and interdependent world creates many conditions that result in crises. In some cases, these are significant events that create widespread harm.

1) Crises are threatening, surprising, and create high levels of uncertainty. They are outside what we consider normal and they require some rapid action to reduce and contain the harm.
2) One of the most important aspects of managing a crisis is communication. Crisis communication is the process of sending and receiving messages between senders and receivers about the risk of a crisis under the extreme conditions of a crisis.
3) A best practices approach to crisis communication follows established guidelines, standards, and generally agreed upon techniques. These have been developed from research and practice and, although they don't include all the answers, they can serve as general recommendations.

References

Federal Emergency Management Agency. (2016). Whole community. http://www.fema.gov/whole-community.

Leitch, S., & Motion, J. (2010). Publics and public relations. In R. Heath (Ed.), *The SAGE handbook of public relations* (pp. 99–110). Thousand Oaks, CA: Sage.

Littlefield, R. S. (2013). 12. Communicating risk and crisis communication to multiple publics. In A. J. DuBrin (Ed.), *Handbook of research on crisis leadership in organizations* (pp. 231–251). Northampton, MA: Edward Elgar Publishing.

Seeger, M. W. (2006). Best practices in crisis communication: An expert panel process. *Journal of Applied Communication Research, 34*(3), 232–244.

Sellnow, T. L., & Seeger, M. W. (2013). *Theorizing crisis communication* (Vol. 4). New York: Wiley.

Steelman, T. A., & McCaffrey, S. (2013). Best practices in risk and crisis communication: Implications for natural hazards management. *Natural Hazards, 65*(1), 683–705.

Taubenberger, J. K., & Morens, D. M. (2006). 1918 influenza: The mother of all pandemics. *Emerging Infectious Diseases.* https://doi.org/10.3201/eid1209.050979

U.S. Department of Homeland Security (2015). Preparedness videos. Retrieved from https://www.ready.gov/videos

Veil, S. R., & Husted, R. A. (2012). Best practices as an assessment for crisis communication. *Journal of Communication Management, 16*(2), 131–145.

2

Process Approach

Take a Process Approach to Crisis Communication

When most people think of a crisis, they think of an explosion, fire, crash, or some other dramatic and damaging event with a definite beginning and a specific end. A crisis is really part of a much longer set of events and factors that occur over an extended period. What we think of as a crisis—the explosion, flood, or disease outbreak—is just one part of a larger process involving the interaction of many factors. Our first best practice suggests that a crisis should not be thought of as a single limited and contained event. Instead, we believe thinking of risks as ongoing issues with the continuous possibility that a particular risk might erupt and become a crisis is far more accurate. This approach also allows managers and public relations professionals to be much more effective in dealing with risks and crises. Because we are constantly surrounded by risks, there is always a chance an emergency or crisis can erupt around us. This does not mean we should constantly be afraid and should not take risks; it simply means we need to work to understand the evolving risks around us and be as prepared as possible.

In this section, we discuss the concept of process and we describe what we mean by a process approach to crisis communication. We also discuss the various stages and phases of a crisis and explore how these can be used to manage risks and crises. Crises generally develop according to patterns and understating the patterns or stages can be very helpful in determining what to communicate, to whom, and when. Finally, we suggest that communication needs to be part of the process of making policy decisions for organizations. Policies in organizations are guidelines for decisions and behaviors and including communication perspectives when policies are created makes them more effective.

Communication in Times of Trouble: Best Practices for Crisis and Emergency Risk Communication, First Edition. Matthew W. Seeger and Timothy L. Sellnow.
© 2019 John Wiley & Sons, Inc. Published 2019 by John Wiley & Sons, Inc.

What Do We Mean by "Communication Is a Process"?

What comes to mind when you think of communication? Is it a message? Perhaps you think of the channel or technology that carries the message, such as a smartphone, radio, or magazine. You might also think of senders and receivers when you think of communication. Senders are often organizations, agencies, or spokespersons. Receivers are often organizational stakeholders, such as customers, suppliers, stockholders, employees, and members of the community as well as other organizations including the media. All these elements, messages, senders, receivers, feedback, and channels go into the larger communication process. A process involves a series of elements, factors, components, or steps that are interacting over time and that lead to outcomes. These interactions also change over time as the conditions and the elements change.

Communication is a process because it involves the dynamic interaction of many components—senders, receivers, messages, channels, feedback, noise—and these components change over time. Senders, for example, change the message as they learn more about a risk or crisis and as the situation develops and evolves. During the communication process, senders and receivers continually adapt to one another, change their messages, acquire new information, change their attitudes, and change their messages as conditions change. Communication is also a process in that it never stops. It is an ongoing and constantly evolving activity. As you send and receive messages from someone, you learn about them and you change how you communicate. In addition, one message sent at one point in time is not sufficient to achieve our goal. Usually, messages need to be repeated and adjusted. Feedback allows messages to be refined and improved. Even the choice not to communicate sometimes can send a message. The statement "no comment" in response to a crisis can send the message that the organization is hiding something or stonewalling. During a crisis, it may create the impression that important information is being withheld, that audiences and issues are being ignored, and that there may be something to hide.

What Does a Process Approach Mean for Crisis?

Crises can also be thought of as processes that create high levels of risk and uncertainty. As society evolves and becomes more complex, the level of risk and uncertainty can also increase. In his important book *Normal Accidents*, Charles Perrow (1984) describes how most crises involve problems with a system made up of many components. Expanding technology has created "tight coupling," or an interdependence of industries, communities, and societies worldwide that intensifies and extends the reach of crises. Problems with a city water supply can affect the quality of parts produced in a manufacturing plant using that water, which can lead to failures in those products. As we move toward a more globalized economy, the risks, economic and otherwise, in one part of the globe have the potential to impact other parts. A recession in China can affect U.S. markets because many U.S. companies sell products to Chinese companies. A conflict in the Middle East may result in increased gasoline prices in the United States. These changes can occur very quickly and, unless managers are paying close attention, their organizations can be caught off guard. Many crises are the consequence of the failure of components or technologies that are part of large complex systems. Small weaknesses in data systems, for example, can result in massive data breaches where personal information is stolen, such as customer social security and credit card numbers. These small weaknesses may not even be evident to the people managing organizations.

One risk that can have very far reaching impacts involves infectious diseases. Some diseases are becoming bigger risks or becoming more common because of changes in society. Several very serious diseases are zoonotic, or diseases that come from animals and somehow jump to humans. These diseases, such as bird flu, can be particularly risky because humans have little or no resistance. Other diseases migrate from one part of the world to others, sometimes hitching a ride through global trade. The Zika virus was originally identified in the Zika forests of Africa in 1946 and has been slowly expanding to tropical areas of the world. It may have been spread to the western hemisphere by people who were unknowingly infected. Now the disease is common throughout South and Central America and is affecting many parts of the United States. Infectious diseases are expected to become very significant risks in the future as travel increases, agriculture practices become more intense, and people live closer together.

Crisis management in this very dynamic and complicated environment requires awareness of the risks associated with complex and changing systems so crises can be avoided when possible. We refer to this kind of awareness as "collective mindfulness." This involves a kind of rich and complex familiarity about the immediate situation that comes from a deep and diverse understanding of the context (Weick, Sutcliffe, & Obstfeld, 2008). Collective mindfulness can also mean depending on experts who understand the risks. It also means all levels of the organization communicate about risks and crises openly and regularly.

As we, or those around us, adopt new technologies and global relationships and work in increasingly complex systems, our objective is to be mindful in ways that help us understand and foresee the potential threats that accompany them. The ability to collect information from multiple sources, anticipate risks, and understand and communicate about them successfully will become an even more valuable skill. A process approach to crisis communication suggests that public relations, marketing, issues management, public affairs, and other communication professionals have a special responsibility in understanding risks and anticipating crises.

Crisis management in these very dynamic and complicated environments also requires that organizations have the capability to respond to a crisis when it occurs, including the ability to continuously communicate effectively as the conditions change. Understanding how risks and crises change over time is necessary for effective crisis communication. Researchers who study crises have pointed out that most crises develop in similar ways and the communication needs change as the crisis evolves. They have identified various stages or phases that are part of the process of crisis development and resolution. We call these stages the crisis life cycle.

What Is a Crisis Life Cycle?

Many descriptions of crisis stages have been developed by researchers. Some of these involve four, five, or six relatively distinct stages of crisis development. The common core in all these depictions can be summarized in three stages: precrisis, crisis, and postcrisis. Precrisis is the stage where risks are developing or incubating. This is a stage for risk assessment and crisis planning. Crisis is the acute stage, where a crisis has erupted and damage (physical or reputational) is occurring and threat is at its highest. Postcrisis is the recovery stage for an organization or community and ushers in a renewed effort toward precrisis planning. From this perspective, the life cycle of a crisis is cyclical, beginning and ending with precrisis assessment and planning. By viewing crisis as a process, we do not treat crises as single events after which we return to *normal*. Rather, we see a crisis as an indication that, on some level, our planning and assessment fell short of our objectives and a "new normal" is needed. By new normal we mean new ways of understanding and managing risks.

The precrisis stage is usually described as an incubation period. During this time, everything appears to be normal. The company, agency, or community is acting in a routine way and there are established behaviors, rules, and procedures for how to avoid any risks. In companies that process food, for example, these may include standards for cleanliness, cooking temperatures, and how food is stored. During this phase, there is some risk factor that is unforeseen, or which goes unnoticed or ignored. For example, there may be a new source of food contamination that isn't understood, such as a new product from a supplier. This new risk factor may interact with a small flaw, such as a refrigeration system that is too warm, and result in a foodborne illness outbreak. Outbreaks of foodborne illness are surprisingly common and can have very significant implications for food companies.

The second phase is the crisis phase, which occurs once the crisis is noticed by a majority of people. Usually, but not always, there is a trigger event in the form of a dramatic occurrence that signals a crisis has started and there is potential for serious harm. This may be an explosion, a report in the media, dramatic rises in flood waters, or many people reporting to local hospitals with illnesses or injuries. During this stage, damage and harm occur to people, property, reputations, organizations, and systems. The crisis stage is usually a very intense time where action must be taken quickly, assistance provided, and information communicated to help contain or limit the harm. If actions are not taken—for example if warnings aren't communicated quickly and effectively—more harm occurs. In the case of a company spilling a dangerous chemical into a river that supplies drinking water, people need to be informed as soon as possible that they should not drink the water. Assistance may be needed and coordinated to provide bottled water and to monitor the river for contamination. Local health care providers need to be informed about the symptoms they may see from people exposed to the chemical. The crisis stage usually continues until there is no new harm occurring.

The postcrisis stage is the time when things begin to return to some level of normal. Although there may still be ongoing cleanup, lawsuits, and lingering questions about what happened, postcrisis is usually a time to take steps to move beyond the crisis. Communities and organizations get back to business. This may involve trying to forget some of the things that happened while documenting and emphasizing others. This is part of learning the lessons of the crisis. In the case of a product defect, such as an ignition switch on cars, company leadership might put new procedures and rules in place to make sure any such defects are identified in the future. These new procedures and rules might be announced publicly to show the organization has moved beyond the crisis. In addition, the postcrisis stage can be an extended period of legal liability and public arguments about blame and responsibility. Sometimes, these arguments can last for years. Questions about blame and responsibility are almost always part of a crisis and most organizations try to resolve these as quickly as possible so they can get on with business. Communication strategies to repair a damaged image are usually part of the effort to get back to normal operations. These strategies can take many forms, including denial, evading responsibility, reducing offensiveness, corrective action, and mortification.

The precrisis, crisis, and postcrisis stages are helpful in determining what needs to be communicated at what points. A crisis can create tremendous uncertainty and knowing what might happen next can help people manage a crisis more successfully. Thinking about a crisis as a series of stages can also help people understand that risk and crisis are parts of an ongoing process and that conditions will change.

How Can These Stages Be Used by Crisis Communicators?

The precrisis, crisis, and post stages can also be very useful in planning communication activities. Each stage creates different communication requirements and, as part of a process approach, messages need to be changed as the crisis evolves.

During the precrisis stage, for example, collecting information about risk factors, how they are developing, and their potential impact is essential. This is an ongoing monitoring activity where information is collected about issues, stakeholders, resources, and the larger environment. Once risks are understood, messages about risk factors and risk avoidance can be developed and communicated. Manufacturing companies often conduct worker safety campaigns with themes such as "Safety First!" and "Safety Is Job One." Precrisis health promotion campaigns may encourage annual influenza vaccinations. Preparedness campaigns may encourage people to "Make a plan and stay informed." In general, planning and preparation are important parts of the precrisis stage and we discuss these in more detail in the next chapter. Precrisis is also a good time to invest in developing positive relationships with stakeholders. These investments can help build up an organization's reservoir of goodwill. This can be thought of as a reputation or image savings account or rainy-day fund that can be used when a crisis is triggered.

The crisis stage is the time when the crisis communication plan is put into action. The plan will require rapid communication designed to reduce uncertainty and contain and limit harm. This includes harm to the organization's image, brands, and reputation. Communicating quickly and coordinating with other groups can help create the impression that the organization is being responsible and is in control of the situation. During the crisis stage, some of the primary channels will be press releases, news conferences, and, increasingly, social media such as Twitter. Social media is a very rapid form of communication and can help get important messages out very quickly. In addition to communicating quickly, it is also important to communicate in ways that are sensitive to any harm that has been created from the crisis. This may involve expressing concern and empathy for those affected and, in some cases, offering apologies. Although organizations are generally very careful not to admit guilt or wrongdoing following a crisis, it is still possible to express concern for those who might have been harmed.

Communication in the final stage, the postcrisis stage, is usually dominated by questions of blame, responsibility, and liability. This is a time for messages that explain what happened and why. In most cases, it is best to get these questions answered in an open and direct way as quickly as possible. Sometimes, questions of cause and blame can linger for months or years as lawsuits are filed and settled. Lingering questions of blame and liability can be ongoing distractions and can become serious threats to an organization's reputation. This can also be a time when the focus shifts to learning the lessons of the crisis and communicating them. Learning is one of the most important functions of postcrisis communication. Lessons can be communicated through executive speeches, at memorial services, and in after action reports (AARs) and can help ensure a similar crisis does not happen again. Sometimes, these lessons can be positive, such as "Our community pulled together to defeat the crisis" or "Our company came out of this crisis more focused on core business." In this way, a crisis sometimes creates the opportunity for learning and improvement and can be a renewing experience. This is determined in part by the communication that occurs in the crisis and postcrisis stages.

The communication required during the stages of crisis also indicates that communication perspectives need to be part of the top decision-making structure of the organization. Key policy decisions about risks and crises need to incorporate communication perspectives from public relations, public affairs, and issue management.

Why Should Communicators Participate in the Policy Formation Process?

The management of risks and crises requires a number of policy decisions. As we described, a policy is a guideline for decisions and actions usually developed by organizations or government agencies. These guidelines can have very broad and long-term implications for how organizations respond to conditions, including crises. Policies, for example, may specify who can serve as a formal spokesperson for certain issues or outline how press releases are approved for final distribution. Policies can also include guidelines for how we respond to a crisis. For example, a policy might specify who will be notified during a crisis, when people might be evacuated, and who has the authority to make those decisions. These guidelines can be especially important during a crisis, where decisions sometimes have to be made very quickly and often without complete information. Some policy decisions can also be made before a crisis erupts, during the precrisis stage, where there is more time to consider many factors. As we discuss in the next chapter, setting out these kinds of policies during precrisis is part of a crisis planning best practice.

Policy decisions can also accelerate effective responses during a crisis. If guidelines are in place about when and how an evacuation order or a recall notice is to be issued, for example, the actual decision can occur more quickly. Usually during a crisis, important decisions have to be made very quickly and often there simply is not time to consult everyone affected, gather information, and consider all the implications. A clear policy about who will be the crisis spokesperson and how messages will be developed and improved can help speed communication to the affected publics. A policy for making decisions during a crisis and communicating them quickly is a best practice.

In many cases, the communication function of an organization is not seen as part of the overall strategic policy formation process. Rather, in many situations, communication is seen as a tactical process for implementing a policy once it has been made (Grunig & Grunig, 2000). The strategic policy process sets the overall direction and goals for an organization and is generally seen as a top management function. In contrast, tactical operations are the day-to-day activities and functions that help carry out or put the strategy in place. To say this another way, tactics can be seen as just announcing a decision once it has been made. When communication is part of the policy formation process, however, the policies usually reflect the needs and interests of audiences and stakeholders. This can be especially important during a crisis where communication is such a central part of the response.

Making sure the communication perspective is represented in the strategic policy process about crises isn't always easy. One of the keys to participating is to ensure communication is part of the larger crisis response function and key crisis management planning and response teams are consulted from the start. In addition, being able to bring useful information about risks and crises to the discussion can help demonstrate the importance of communication to crisis management. As we discussed earlier, the precrisis stage should include monitoring for issues and threats. Public relations and communication can demonstrate the value of these activities by collecting and distributing that information to other decision makers. During the crisis stage, public relations and communication staff can show their value by formulating the initial response and anticipating next steps. In postcrisis, making sure lessons are described, disseminated, and acted on can also help demonstrate that communication should be part of the policy process.

Summary

Crises are becoming increasingly complex as our organizations and society evolve. We are constantly exposed to risk on many levels. We are continuously in a precrisis state until we experience a full-blown emergency or crisis. We move from crisis to postcrisis recovery and back to precrisis. For these reasons, crisis is best seen as an ongoing process where we are always moving from a circumstance we consider normal to what we recognize as a new normal. Thinking about crisis in this way is a best practice that helps us prepare, anticipate, and respond. Crisis communication also functions best when it is part of the strategic policy making process.

Key Takeaways for a Process Approach to Crisis Communication

1) Communication is a dynamic process where many elements, factors, and components interact over time. We adapt and change our messages to meet evolving conditions, which helps improve the effectiveness of our communication.

2) A crisis often involves the interaction of many different interdependent systems and this may extend the impact of a crisis far beyond the immediate context. Understanding the potential for extended impact requires mindfulness.

3) Part of understanding crisis as a process means understanding how the crisis develops over time through a series of stages or phases. Many researchers describe three phases: precrisis, crisis, and postcrisis. Each stage requires different communication activities.

4) Policy decisions about risk and crisis management are most effective when they incorporate a communication perspective. Communication should be treated as a core management function in organizations.

References

Grunig, J. E., & Grunig, L. A. (2000). Public relations in strategic management and strategic management of public relations: Theory and evidence from the IABC excellence project. *Journalism Studies, 1*(2), 303–321.

Perrow, C. (1984). *Normal accidents: Living with high risk technologies.* Princeton, NJ: Princeton University Press.

Weick, K. E., Sutcliffe, K. M., & Obstfeld, D. (2008). Organizing for high reliability: Processes of collective mindfulness. *Journal of Contingencies and Crisis Management, 3*(1), 81–123.

3

Preevent Planning
Engage in Preevent Planning for Crisis Communication

A second crisis communication best practice is preevent planning. Planning the response to a possible crisis is one of the most important steps in creating an effective response. In general, planning is most effective when it is an ongoing process rather than a specific one-time outcome or document. Although we recommend having a crisis plan on the shelf, having a plan does not necessarily ensure an effective response. The plan must be updated and, when needed, executed correctly. Planning does have a variety of benefits, including identifying areas of risk and making efforts to reduce them, presetting the initial crisis responses so decision making during a crisis is more efficient, and identifying necessary resources to respond. These resources include people, information, skills, and materials. In addition, analyzing and assessing the most likely risks are important for crisis prevention and management.

What Does Planning Involve?

Planning is something we all do. It is a process of thinking about and anticipating what might need to happen to achieve a desired outcome or goal. Planning to cook dinner involves developing a menu, determining ingredients, anticipating how many people will be eating, and working out the timing of the cooking. Planning is necessary to prepare a good dinner. Planning is also part of our everyday efforts in almost all our activities, such as studying, traveling, shopping, exercising, and even our recreation. Planning also allows us to avoid undesirable outcomes by avoiding risks. Many drivers use applications on their mobile devices to avoid road construction or accidents. Anticipating the onset of flu season may result in a plan to get a flu shot, thus reducing the risk of getting sick.

Communication in Times of Trouble: Best Practices for Crisis and Emergency Risk Communication, First Edition. Matthew W. Seeger and Timothy L. Sellnow.
© 2019 John Wiley & Sons, Inc. Published 2019 by John Wiley & Sons, Inc.

Forethought, or the process of projecting and anticipating through advanced consideration, is the heart of effective planning.

Companies and agencies use planning as a way to reduce their uncertainty, or the degree to which they can anticipate and control outcomes. When uncertainty is high, they have little idea what might happen next. In the introduction, we described the fact that uncertainty is one of the defining characteristics of a crisis. A crisis creates high levels of uncertainty because the things we rely on to create a sense of normal and predict outcomes are suddenly disrupted. Most organizations rely on established routines to conduct business. Employees show up to work at a specific time and place. They are working with people they know, doing tasks they are familiar with, using equipment they know how to operate. Following a severe weather event or a fire, offices may be damaged or inaccessible. Computers may be destroyed and important records lost. Some employees may be hurt or missing. An alternative location may be necessary for the company to continue to do business. Backup records may be accessed from remote locations. Temporary employees may be hired to fill vacant positions. In the case of an accusation of management misconduct or a product that appears to be defective, management of the organization can't determine what the impact might be. Will the product need to be recalled? Will the company be sued? Will top management be forced to resign? In these cases, having a plan in place for top management succession or for notifying customers of a defective produce can reduce uncertainty and the possible negative impact of a crisis.

Have you ever considered what you would do if something bad happened? How would you get out of your house if there was a fire and where would you go? This plan would involve an evacuation route and an assembly place so everyone can be accounted for after an evacuation. What would you do if someone came into your classroom with a gun and threatened to shoot people? A planned response in this case would most likely involve calling or notifying police, assessing the situation, sheltering in place and perhaps barricading a door, and, when it is safe, evacuating. This approach of **c**all, **a**ssess, **s**helter, and **e**vacuate is called CASE and is an easy way to plan a response. Crisis planning is a process that an individual, group, organization, or community can undertake to anticipate and prepare for a threatening and surprising situation. Crisis planning involves setting in place initial actions and ways to determine what to do and how to respond.

There are many types of crisis plans. Evacuation plans are necessary whenever a crisis or risk can have an impact on a specific location, such as a large office building, hotel, theater, school, or stadium. Building evacuation plans generally specify safe routes and procedures and indicate what kinds of warnings and alerts would signal an evacuation. For most large buildings, evacuation plans are posted in prominent locations and people are told to use stairs not elevators because many crises create power outages, stranding people in elevators. Continuity of operations planning, according to the Federal Emergency Management Agency (FEMA), is designed to ensure the continuation of essential business or organizational functions. "In order to achieve that goal, the objective for organizations is to identify their Essential Functions (EFs) and ensure that those functions can be continued throughout, or resumed rapidly after, a disruption of normal activities" (FEMA, 2016, para. 1). These essential functions may include protecting critical records, taking and processing orders, or taking care of clients and employees.

What Is Crisis Communication Planning?

According to the Institute of Public Relations, "Crisis management is a process designed to prevent or lessen the damage a crisis can inflict on an organization and its stakeholders" (2007, para. 4). Crisis communication planning is a very important part of the overall crisis management process. Quite simply, it is not possible to manage a crisis without communication and communication is often the primary response to a crisis. This includes determining what information to communicate, in what way, when, and to what audiences.

When we suggest that crisis planning is a process, we mean it involves several ongoing activities that include many parts of the organization, from top management on down. Usually, a crisis plan is thought of as a product—a document, or series of templates, filed away under the heading "In case of an emergency." In fact, there are many companies and public relations agencies that essentially sell a prepackaged crisis communication plan. These plans often do not meet the specific needs of an organization. When a crisis plan is treated as a process, the specific needs and risks of that organization are addressed. Process also means the plan will exist as a living document that is regularly updated and that the plan will be regularly rehearsed. There are many cases where an organization facing a crisis activates its plan only to discover it is out of date, personnel have changed, e-mail addresses are no longer accurate, or resources are no longer available. In one case, important crisis response equipment designated for an oil spill had been loaned to another group and never returned. When managers and public relations staff participate in planning, they have the chance to think systematically about the various risks the organization faces. This "what if" exercise can be very valuable in identifying and correcting points of vulnerability. Finally, process suggests ongoing attention to issues of risks and crisis by all parts of the organization.

A crisis communication plan does, however, usually include a document or series of documents. Sometimes crisis plans are kept in portable external drives that are password protected. Hard copies are also recommended because they can be accessed even without electricity or computers. The plan is usually developed by a crisis committee or team and is updated, tested, and rehearsed regularly, at least once every 2 years. The Public Relations Society of America (2016) says a crisis plan should have seven characteristics:

1) Top management approval and support should be in place before the planning process starts.
2) Plans should be grounded in a sensible and sound strategy.
3) Plans should provide guidance for the first few minutes and the first few hours of a crisis event.
4) Plans should include the management of media coverage and public concerns about the victims, from the start of the crisis.
5) Management should be involved meaningfully in both readiness and execution of the plan.
6) The plan should accommodate the foreseeable patterns of mistakes, problems, and distractions.
7) The plan should emphasize accountable, ethical, and moral behavior by leaders.

These characteristics help ensure a crisis communication plan is connected to the rest of the organization. They also address some of the basic communication issues that almost always arise in a crisis.

How Is a Plan Created?

As we noted, a crisis communication plan is usually developed by a committee or team. One of the first decisions that must be made is whether the crisis communication plan should be part of a larger crisis response plan or be separate. A crisis communication plan that is part of a larger crisis plan can get lost in the larger effort to respond to a crisis—but making it part of the larger plan can help ensure good coordination. A separate communication plan can help make sure all the communication issues are worked out, but it can also create coordination issues. The specific conditions of the organization and the risks will determine if a separate communication plan is the best approach.

The second decision concerns who should be on the planning team. If the effort is to create a general crisis plan, the team should include most of the people who will respond to the crisis, but it might also include others with specific expertise or skills. Senior managers, preferably the chief executive officer, should participate in the planning. The senior communications staff from marketing, public relations, and public affairs should participate on the team. If the organization has a security department, their participation is also critical, as well as the legal department. Representatives from key operations areas such as manufacturing, distribution, and human resources should also be present.

Many issues of crisis communication plans will be determined by the nature of the organization, where it is located, its size, and its operations. Some organizations, such as hospitals, schools, and airlines, are mandated to address specific kinds of threats. Schools, for example, have to be prepared for active shooters, fires, and severe weather. Most of us remember fire drills from school. These drills are required by state and federal law. Airlines are required to have certain safety equipment in place and personnel are trained in emergency response. One reason organizations in these industries are required to have crisis response plans is because the risks are clear and these kinds of crises happen often. Determining what risks an organization faces is another important step in developing a crisis plan.

How Is Risk Assessed?

When organizations begin to plan for crisis, they must consider the types of risks they face. These risks are a function of the industry, location, processes, and context. Some risks are a function of the industry. Manufacturing organizations face industrial accidents, fires, and explosions. Chemical companies risk spills, as do the oil industry and many transportation organizations. The food industry regularly experiences cases of foodborne illness due to contamination. Carefully researching the kinds of crises competitors have experienced is one way to determine industry-specific risks. Risk may also come from location. The Midwest experiences tornadoes. The U.S. Gulf Coast is prone to hurricanes. The northeast United States is regularly hit with extreme blizzards. Other parts of the country experience flooding, wildfires, earthquakes, and mudslides. Drought is a much more serious risk for many parts of the country, including the west and southwest. Climate change has increased many of the location-specific risks for organizations and they are likely to become even more severe. The processes used by organizations can also be sources of risk. Some manufacturing and construction are inherently dangerous. Some organizations work with very dangerous chemicals and materials—including radioactive substances and disease organisms. These need to be considered in developing crisis plans. Finally, the overall context of the organization should be taken into account. Multinational organizations, for example, have to plan for crises under a wide array of conditions with different laws, regulatory agencies, and reporting requirements. Very diverse and engaged stakeholders and controversial public policy issues can also be sources of risks.

All organizations should identify potential risks and hazards and work to reduce them, even after the plan is complete. Sometimes this involves establishing new systems and procedures. For example, Hazard Analysis Critical Control Point plans are used to manage the risk of foodborne illness. In this approach, the specific points, processes, or procedures for a possible food contamination are identified and managed. This may involve handwashing stations at critical points or chemical disinfectants for some equipment. Having a plan and a planning process in place serve as constant reminders of potential problems and provide checkpoints for employees to follow in hopes of preventing crises. Such planning, therefore, can enhance overall mindfulness regarding risks.

What Is Included in a Crisis Plan?

Many organizations and agencies have crisis communication planning templates, including the FEMA Community Planning template and the Centers for Disease Control and Prevention's Crisis and Emergency Risk Communication template. These models generally outline what should be included in a plan and how the planning process should progress. They can be very helpful resources in developing a crisis communication plan. The plan usually takes the form of a document or electronic file that outlines the initial response to a crisis, identifies responsibilities, and includes various resources, such as contact lists, templates, and draft press releases. A crisis communication plan should include several elements.

The first part of a crisis plan is usually a statement from top management that includes the organization's primary approach or philosophy in responding to a crisis. This can be a value statement, a statement of principles, or a statement about priorities. These kinds of clear messages by top management can be very important during the uncertainty and stress of a crisis. For example, a clear statement about the importance of customer safety and well-being can be very helpful in determining how to respond to a crisis involving a defective product. A statement about the importance of honesty in responding to a crisis can help avoid the tendency to deceive or "spin" a crisis.

The second part of a crisis communication plan is a clear indication of who is responsible for activating the plan. In other words, what factors may signal a crisis and who can say when a crisis has actually occurred? In many cases, such as a fire, chemical leak, workplace shooting, or severe weather event, activation is usually very obvious. In other cases, such as a defective product or management misconduct, the need for activation may not be as clear. In these cases, some person must be designated to initiate the crisis plan. This typically means calling the crisis team together.

A third part of a crisis communication plan specifies the members of the crisis communication team and their various responsibilities. As described earlier, this includes representatives from marketing, public relations, operations, legal affairs, spokespersons, senior management, as well as others, depending on the nature of the organization. In outlining responsibilities of team members, the plan specifies who is responsible for what and what tools (press conferences, media interviews, e-mail, voicemail, intranet, news release, Twitter, Facebook, company web pages, etc.) will be used. Who will monitor social media? Who will be responsible for community relations, customer relations, government relations? Which member of the team will serve as spokesperson? How will the team respond to inquiries?

At the heart of a crisis communication plan is a set of activities and procedures that need to be undertaken to manage the crisis. The fourth component of a crisis communication plan should describe step-by-step procedures for both internal and external communication. How will messages be developed and approved? How will feedback be collected, from whom, and how will it be used? How will the impact of the crisis be tracked? Will the media be monitored and by whom? What are the company policies and procedures regarding employee or customer privacy, access to needed resources, and notification of others, such as community members, law enforcement, and regulatory agencies? In the case that people are harmed, what resources will be available?

A fifth component of a crisis communication plan is the development of key messages for the kinds of risks that are faced by that organization. As described earlier, schools regularly face and prepare for extreme weather events. Key messages and procedures for canceling school should be part of school plans along with weather drills for events such as tornadoes. Sadly, they also increasingly face cases of violence, including active shootings. Most schools now rehearse active shooter drills as well as standard messages for parents, media, and members of the community for school drills, lockdowns, and actual events. These messages may take the form of draft press releases, draft statements from senior management, or basic frequently asked questions. Background information about the company should also be prepared. Having these draft messages prepared in advance helps make sure things are not missed and messages are developed in a thoughtful way without the intense time pressure of a crisis. When a crisis actually occurs, the messages are adapted to that specific event. In developing key messages, the plan should also describe the various audiences that need to be addressed. Most crises will affect a wide range of people beyond the usual audience of customers, employees, and suppliers. Members of the community, victims, and the family members of victims, local officials, as well as members of any boards or governing groups should also be included in plans for notification. As described earlier, for some kinds of crises, such as chemical spills or food contamination, regulations require that various agencies be notified.

Beyond notification, coordination is one of the most important parts of crisis communication and the crisis plan should include a wide range of contact information for internal and external groups. These include local, state, and national media; community groups; key customers; suppliers; industry groups; support agencies (such as the Red Cross); health care facilities; government; and regulatory agencies. Contacts for internal audiences, including key employees, union leaders, members of the board, and all senior management, should also be in the plan. Cell phone numbers, e-mail addresses, and even phone numbers for vacation homes should be in the plan. Coordination can also be helped through the use of a joint information center (JIC) where representatives from all the groups and organizations engaged in a response meet to ensure their messages are consistent with one another. The JIC is used extensively by crisis response groups and government agencies. Crisis communicators and public information officers meet in a central location to develop messages for the general public as well as specialized groups. Any differences in what is to be communicated are worked out in advance. The JIC can help disseminate accurate, coordinated, and consistent messages.

Standard Elements of a Crisis Communication Plan

1) Statement of support by top management along with statement of priorities, values, and principles. Statement should include purpose of the plan and why the plan is needed.
2) Activation responsibility and criteria: Identify who can activate the plan and under what circumstances.
3) Crisis communication team members.
4) Procedures: Outline the steps that need to be taken regarding internal and external communication, including who is responsible for what and what tools (e-mail, voicemail, intranet, news release, Twitter, etc.) will be used to carry out the plan.
5) Key messages.

6) Contacts and media lists.
7) Schedule for rehearsing, drills, and exercises.
8) Additional information and resources.

The crisis communication plan should also include information about rehearsals, drills, and exercises so the plan can be tested and updated as needed. Drills and exercises can include training, such as preparing spokespersons for speaking to the media or preparing employees to respond to calls on a crisis hotline. Exercises can also demonstrate gaps or deficiencies in the plan, such as who has been left out of the notification system or what aspects of media monitoring have not been covered. Exercises and drills often identify problems in coordinating responses. Exercises may also be called tabletop drills, where members of the crisis teams talk through what they would do during a crisis and various scenarios are described. Full crisis drills are simulations and may include people playing the part of victims and the media. In some cases, journalists are invited to cover the drill as a news item.

Crisis communication plans should include structures that allow for regular updates and revisions and as well as a regular schedule for revising the plan. This should include a schedule for updating, meeting dates for the crisis committee, and opportunities to accommodate new understandings about risk, new partners, and new response contingencies. For this reason, information-sharing networks are effective and efficient ways of obtaining new insights that can then be incorporated into the planning process. Crisis communicators should be willing to share the lessons they learned with others, including other communication and public relations professionals.

A final section of the crisis communication plan is a place for additional information that may be needed. The company mission statement, recent executive speeches, and the contact information for industry groups can all be important resources during a crisis. Having this information in the crisis communication plan helps make a response easier and faster.

Implementing a Crisis Plan

Ideally, a company will never need to use its crisis plan. In many cases, developing the plan helps the organization avoid crises. Even if the company does have a crisis, a plan that was carefully developed by involving many members and is exercised and updated regularly may not be pulled off the shelf because everyone knows what to do. Realistically, every organization and company will experience a crisis and the plan will need to be implemented.

A crisis communication plan is a general outline of a crisis response. As such, it must be adapted to the specifics of the situation. This means assessing the specific conditions of the crisis by collecting as much real-time information as possible through such efforts as media monitoring, including social media; visiting the location of the crisis; and speaking with those most affected by the crisis. Many organizations will also conduct opinion surveys during a crisis to determine how the events are affecting their reputation and brands. Although there is a tendency for managers to withdraw during a crisis and avoid sharing information, openness is critical to implementing the crisis plan. Some important questions to ask are: Does the scale of the crisis or the level of harm exceed our capacity? Are unanticipated groups involved in the crisis? Have we experienced a similar crisis in the past? Do we have the necessary resources to manage this crisis? How long do we expect this crisis to last?

In addition, crises almost always develop in unexpected ways. Unforeseen harm occurs. Secondary crises happen. Personnel are harmed, in some cases seriously, and are unavailable. Facilities, records, and equipment are destroyed or are inaccessible. Flexibility and improvisation are critical in these circumstances. Plans need to be thought of as general guidelines that can be adjusted as circumstances change.

Summary

Organizations and agencies benefit from precrisis planning. Having a plan in place reduces the time needed to form and enact a response to a crisis or emergency. The features of these plans should be based on a process of risk analysis that is appropriate for the organization. Templates for such planning are already available from a variety of industries and government agencies. Having a crisis communication plan does not ensure success but it does increase the chances the company will know what to say and how to say it.

Key Takeaways for Preevent Planning

1) Planning involves anticipating what might happen during a crisis and determining how an organization might respond. A plan is a general outline rather than a specific step-by-step set of activities because the conditions of a crisis cannot always be anticipated.

2) Planning can begin by assessing the kinds of crises that have occurred in the past, considering specific risks associated with an industry or location, and thinking about what crises other organizations have

faced. Not all risks can be anticipated, which is why it is best to plan generally.

3) Crisis plans should be updated regularly and crisis exercises should be used to test the plan and help train people. This helps ensure the plan is current and everyone is familiar with their responsibilities.

4) Plans incorporate many elements, including identifying specific responsibilities of employees and important resources; identifying and describing stakeholders and audiences; specifying channels of communication; and providing general outlines for messages. Also important are various policies for releasing messages, maintaining privacy, creating consistent messages through a JIC, and determining who will serve as spokesperson.

5) Crisis plans can't ensure a crisis won't happen or that a crisis will be managed successfully. A plan does, however, increase the chances a crisis will be managed successfully.

References

Federal Emergency Management Agency. (2016). *What is continuity of operations?* [Brochure]. Retrieved from https://www.fema.gov/pdf/about/org/ncp/coop_brochure.pdf

Institute for Public Relations. (2007, October 30). Crisis management and communications. Retrieved from http://www.instituteforpr.org/crisis-management-and-communications

Public Relations Society of America. (2016) Elements of a crisis plan. New York, NY: PRSA.

4

Partnerships

Form Stakeholder Partnerships with Publics

A third best practice in crisis communication relates to communicating with publics to form partnerships in preventing, managing, and recovering from crises. Publics have the right to know what is happening in a high-risk or crisis situation and organizations managing crises have a responsibility to share this information. This public communication includes messages from government response agencies and companies associated with the risk or crisis. Within this communication obligation are specific implications for the timely and accurate exchange of information, including both sharing and soliciting concerns and questions with publics. Ideally, publics can serve as a resource rather than a burden in risk and crisis management. Risk and crisis communication best practices emphasize creating a shared dialog between the groups and organizations managing a risk or crisis and publics affected by a risk or crisis.

Why Do Crisis Leaders Sometimes Avoid Communicating With Their Publics?

One of the reasons many crisis managers avoid communicating openly during a crisis is the myth that accurate information about a crisis will cause publics to panic (Sheppard, Rubin, Wardman, & Wessely, 2006). Despite the belief that people panic during crisis, this myth is not supported by research. In fact, there is some reason to believe the opposite is true. Withholding information from publics decreases the probability of an appropriate response (Herovic, Sellnow, & Anthony, 2014).

A second reason organizations often avoid communicating is the uncertainty about what to say (Reynolds & Seeger, 2005). By their nature, crises always include some uncertainty. At the onset of a crisis, what is happening is not fully understood. Uncertainty about what will happen

Communication in Times of Trouble: Best Practices for Crisis and Emergency Risk Communication, First Edition. Matthew W. Seeger and Timothy L. Sellnow.
© 2019 John Wiley & Sons, Inc. Published 2019 by John Wiley & Sons, Inc.

next results in uncertainty about how to respond. If, however, crisis communicators wait to address their publics until they have a complete understanding of the crisis, the delay will create frustration and diminishing confidence. Waiting for all the facts to come in before communication will encourage audiences to seek out and accept information from less credible (or completely untrustworthy) sources.

Finally, some organizational leaders believe it is safer to avoid being open and honest during a crisis. Attorneys sometimes advise leaders to say as little as possible and may even suggest what is essentially a "no comment" approach. Although such a response may help protect the company from greater legal trouble in the postcrisis phase, it can be very damaging to the organization's long-term reputation. Taking a "no comment" approach simply creates the impression the company has something to hide.

How Are Relationships With Publics Established?

The time to establish relationships with publics is now—well before the onset of the crisis. A number of studies have found that establishing positive relationships with stakeholders and creating a reservoir of goodwill *before* an event is critical to the successful management of a crisis (Ulmer, Sellnow, & Seeger, 2015). Ongoing interaction with publics is necessary for creating this credibility. In addition, the credibility an organization develops prior to a crisis is particularly valuable during a crisis. Organizations that fail to develop credible relationships prior to a crisis will have a much more difficult time doing so after a crisis occurs. In fact, lack of credibility may significantly increase the level of harm.

The best practice of forming partnerships with publics, however, extends far beyond simply sharing information. The word "partnership" implies much more than a one-way declaration of facts and corresponding strategies relayed by those with expertise or authority related to risks and crises. Partnerships, as we discuss in detail later, require that communication operates as a transaction between organizations or government agencies and their publics. For true partnerships to form, these transactions must reach the level of dialog.

Government agencies have long realized the limits of one-way communication in managing risk. This linear view of communication leaves publics without the opportunity to share their reactions, recommendations, and concerns about how the situation is being managed. Most important, the linear view prohibits the establishment of partnerships with publics. Recognizing the inadequacy of linear communication, the

National Research Council (NRC) conducted an extensive study of risk communication in the 1980s (1989). The study resulted in a report titled, "Risk Assessment in the Federal Government: Managing the Process." The report noted an inadequacy of risk communication research. In response to this need, the NRC formed the Committee on Risk Perception and Communication. This committee published the groundbreaking book *Improving Risk Communication* in 1989. In this book, the NRC endorsed a view of risk communication as a "democratic dialog" (1989, p. 21). The following definition of risk communication provided in the book is a mainstay in the practice of risk communication:

> Risk communication is an interactive process of exchange of information and opinion among individuals, groups, and institutions. It involves multiple messages about the nature of risk and other messages, not strictly about risk, that express concerns, opinions, or reaction to risk messages or to legal or institutional arrangements for risk management. (p. 21)

This definition establishes dialog, two-way communication, and mutual exchange as the goal of risk communication. As we discuss next, true interactive dialog with publics is not possible without forming partnerships.

What Is Dialog?

The study of dialog dates to the ancient Greeks. The most familiar reference is to dialog in the so-called Socratic method of teaching. A Socratic dialog involves a process of shared discovery among people, often a teacher and student, based on a series of analytical questions relevant to a specific topic. From this inception, dialog is now a central focus for studying relationships, ethics, and decision making. Unfortunately, dialog is often mistaken for conversation. In fact, organizations often use the term dialog to describe communication settings where some form of simple feedback is provided by publics. In their formative work, Kent and Taylor (1998) established the five principles for dialog involving an organization and its publics:

1) In dialog, organizations and agencies accept that there is a *risk* that the communication transaction with their publics can result in the revision or outright rejection of its conclusions and recommendations.
2) All parties must see each other with a sense of *mutuality* or equality. For example, the needs of the organization do not supersede the needs of a community of residents.

3) A sense of *propinquity* or relationship must be present among all parties engaged in dialog. Without a sense that an ongoing relationship exists and will continue to exist, the communication is linear in nature.

4) Dialog requires *empathy*. Those involved in the communication exchange must value the good of the others in the relationship. The need for empathy rules out any communication strategy that does not account for the good of the other party.

5) Finally, dialog requires a *commitment* to maintaining the conversation. Parties involved in dialog may reach goals and milestones, but there remains a commitment to ongoing communication that attends to evolving needs.

In short, people do not reach the level of true dialog unless they value the relationship, seek the best for the other parties, and are willing to adapt their policies and behaviors based on mutual respect for ideas shared and for the emotions experienced by all. Clearly, organizations and agencies cannot possibly reach the level of dialog promoted by the NRC if they engage in linear, one-way communication.

Why Do Some Agencies and Organizations Fail to Establish Dialog?

A helpful strategy for successfully achieving dialog with publics is to understand how other agencies and organizations consistently fail to do so. The primary cause of failure to reach the level of dialog occurs because of a misinterpretation or lack of knowledge about what is true dialog. For example, some organizations are apprehensive about dialog because they believe such interaction as an invitation for publics to vent by expressing their anger, disapproval, or lack of trust in the organization. Such expressions indeed may occur, but avoiding or discounting these kinds of interactions precludes the opportunity to initiate dialog. A related temptation is to misinterpret dialog as customer service where two-way communication is used simply and briefly to negotiate a resolution (or lack thereof) stemming from a customer complaint (Kent & Theunissen, 2016). Simple two-way communication does not create the partnerships we believe in this best practice of crisis communication.

Others may see publics as incapable of comprehending the complexity of the science or data the organization is using to make decisions. In doing so, the organization assumes a paternalistic or power relationship over publics based on their expertise or knowledge. Both assumptions are invitations for failure. Condescending assumptions about one's audience make achieving mutual respect impossible. The key challenge for those who wish to establish a dialog with their publics is translating complex information at a highly practical level so publics can understand the risk and how that risk applies to them and their loved ones. As Kent and Lane (2017) explain, in dialog, information is shared in a way that can "appeal to publics" and make them "partners in naming the world" (p. 572). This process of translation cannot succeed unless organizations continue the dialog by consistently taking into account feedback and revising the message until it is both comprehendible and sufficient to meet the needs of listeners. For example, organizers of the Great ShakeOut—a campaign encouraging Americans to participate in earthquake drills teaching them to drop, cover, and hold on during earthquakes—regularly asks for feedback from people participating in the drill. Organizers of the ShakeOut frequently revise the content and means for distributing ShakeOut messages based on this sincere effort to better understand concerns of publics about and comprehension of earthquake readiness messages.

Dialog is also impossible if organizations see themselves as holding a power position over their publics. By a power relationship, we mean that an organization exerts or assumes to exert some level of control over a group or community. Naturally, there are times when an authoritative function is essential. For example, agencies may prohibit access to areas where extreme threat exists or where evacuated homes are left unattended for a period. In the ongoing exchange of information focused on risks or crisis recovery, however, coercive messages or actions are inappropriate. Dialog, by its nature, cannot be based on power. Rather, dialog results in "long lasting relationships nurtured, sought, and undertaken with humility and an understanding that the purpose of the conversation is not to get one's way, but to truly understand and gain deeper knowledge" (Kent & Theunissen, 2016, p. 4042).

How Does Dialog Produce Partnerships With Publics?

Because dialog stresses the development of an ongoing and lasting relationship, it is best thought of as a product where genuine relationships exist rather than simply a strategic process or strategy (Kent & Taylor, 1998). In this case, the relational product is a partnership that engages the organization and its publics in a coordinated effort to manage risks and respond to crises. Thus, engagement and the partnerships naturally emerging from this interaction are an inherent outgrowth of dialog (Taylor & Kent, 2014). For such engaged partnerships to develop, organizations must be attuned to and willing to tailor and adjust their messages for subgroups within the larger audience of publics. A single message to a mass audience, although potentially helpful as a warning, does not create dialog and engaged partnerships (Lane & Kent, 2018). Rather, messages tailored for and refined through interactions with subgroups, initiated by any of the parties involved, can help create the partnerships we advocate (Sellnow, Sellnow, Lane, & Littlefield, 2012). Because we want the best for our partners in dialog, organizations emphasize sharing protective actions—not only for individuals but for their families and communities as well. Thus, the crucial purpose of engaged dialog in a risk and crisis setting is never to simply benefit the organization. The goal is always the safety and well-being of all publics served by the organization. Because of the rich potential for creating partnerships that can minimize harm and save lives, we share Kent and Lane's (2017) view that "dialog should be an organizational ethic rather than a strategic tool" (p. 576).

Are There Times When Dialog Should Be Avoided?

The partnerships created through dialog are valuable at all points in risk or crisis situations. There are moments in the acute phase of a crisis where the form of communication may shift more to instruction than the give-and-take approach of interaction (Sellnow & Sellnow, 2010). The acute phase of a crisis is when the risk of injury, damage, or loss of reputation are highest. During hurricanes, for example, the acute phase begins when the storm is nearing landfall and ends when the storm dissipates. At this point, the risk has become a crisis, and the time for exchanging messages is limited. Accordingly, the messages shared by state governments and federal agencies must focus on specific instructions. These instructions might be to evacuate specific areas or building types, such as mobile or manufactured homes. Other instructions may be to shelter in place with enough water, nonperishable food, flashlights, and alternate sources of electricity (such as batteries and generators) on hand to last for several days.

These instructions for self-protection may seem linear or unidirectional with the agencies speaking and the residents listening. For a comparatively brief phase of the initial crisis, this may be true. Instructions for protective action cannot reach their full potential for effectiveness, however, without dialog taking place before and immediately following the most intense moments of the crisis. The sense of partnership instilled through dialog makes individuals more likely to comply with the recommended instructions for self-protection, particularly when individuals feel the messages are tailored to their specific needs and the needs of their communities (Noar, Benac, & Harris, 2007; Sellnow et al., 2012). In a later section, we provide more detail on messages that empower publics to protect themselves during crises.

What Roles Can Publics Play in Their Partnerships With Organizations and Agencies?

There are many examples of community partnerships aiding in the prevention and management of crises. A compelling example of such successful community partnerships throughout the United States is the Department of Homeland Security's "If you see something, say something" program. The overriding philosophy of the program that began in 2010 is, "It takes a community to protect a community" (Department of Homeland Security, n.d., para. 1). The nationwide campaign raises public awareness about possible signs of terrorist-related crime. The objective is to encourage people to notice suspicious behavior and report their observations to the nearest supervisory officials or call 911. In many cases, community residents are most likely to notice when something unusual is happening in the places they live or frequently visit. The program helps travelers at major facilities and en route to their destinations; students, faculty, and staff at schools on all levels; fans at sporting events and concerts; shoppers at busy stores; and people outside their homes for many other reasons learn to notice and report unattended bags, troubling conversations, or any other signs of potentially threatening behaviors. These partnerships give community officials thousands of added eyes and ears to help detect and prevent potential attacks.

The National Crime Prevention Council's Neighborhood Watch program is another formalized example of a community partnership. The program, originally launched in 1972, was designed to train and organize residents to assist law enforcement agencies in keeping a watchful eye on their neighborhoods (National Crime Prevention Council, n.d.). Residents participating in the program coordinate with their police and sheriffs' offices, participate in training, link with victim's services, attend regular neighborhood meetings, recruit new members, and many other activities relevant to the needs of their neighborhood residents. Although these programs are extremely helpful in controlling crime, they can also adapt quickly to fulfill other neighborhood needs in response to crises of almost any kind.

Partnerships can also arise spontaneously, which is often a characteristic of a crisis. After Hurricane Harvey left people in many areas of the Houston community trapped in their flooded neighborhoods, scores of volunteers offered to use their boats and other crafts to help evacuate stranded citizens and their pets. Officials in the flooded city welcomed the volunteers after recognizing the added resources were needed to cope with the unprecedented need. To further help coordinate the volunteer activities, other citizens formed impromptu organizations using social media to help identify those in need and recruit volunteer rescuers (Rincon, 2017). This willingness to serve and the capacity for citizen-created organizations to emerge almost instantly is a pattern observed in other crises as well. For example, when hundreds of thousands of people were left with unsafe drinking water after a chemical spill in the Charleston, W.Va., area, volunteers both within the community and concerned citizens outside the state formed emergent organizations to help give residents the information they needed to access water and eventually flush the contaminated water from their homes (Getchell, 2017). Community partnerships such as those forming in Houston and West Virginia contribute remarkably to postcrisis recovery.

Citizens have also instinctively collaborated in emergency situations to stop crises in progress. The most vivid examples of this immediate alliance have occurred on passenger aircraft. For example, in the case of the so-called "shoe bomber," airline passengers in 2001 noticed and responded when another passenger attempted to ignite explosives hidden in his shoes. Similarly, in 2009, passengers responded when they observed an individual trying to detonate explosives hidden in his underwear. In both cases, potential disasters were averted ("Passengers help," 2009). Passengers and observers have also spontaneously taken heroic actions in other settings. Three Americans on a crowded train from Amsterdam to Paris helped thwart a mass shooting. The Americans tackled a heavily armed shooter as he tangled momentarily with another French citizen. A shooter on the campus of Seattle Pacific University killed one student and wounded another outside before entering a building and wounding a second student. As the shooter attempted to reload his weapon, another student sprayed the shooter with pepper spray, wrestled his weapon from him, and subdued the shooter until help arrived (Green, 2016). In each of these examples, individuals responded instantaneously to prevent horrible consequences.

Each of these examples of community partnerships involves dialog. The "If you see something, say something" campaign promotes dialog among citizens and protective agencies. The Neighborhood Watch program encourages dialog among local law enforcement agencies and communities. The airline passengers who acted spontaneously to disrupt potential bombers did so with knowledge and recommendations shared broadly after the 9/11 hijackings. Likewise, the student who stopped the shooter at Seattle Pacific University had been exposed to the sad consequences of other campus shootings and he was trained as a building safety monitor. This exposure invites citizens to participate in an ongoing dialog about how to respond to these dangerous events. As these examples clearly illustrate, citizens can and do capitalize on dialog in ways that contribute to their safety and the safety of others around them.

Summary

Forming partnerships with publics creates opportunities for these populations to serve as a resource to assist in managing the crisis. Although some organizations are tempted to avoid sharing the information needed to form such partnerships due to fears of litigation, doing so can boost an organization's credibility and effectiveness in managing the crisis. Community groups, such as the Neighborhood Watch program, and national campaigns such as "If you see something, say something" could not exist without an ongoing dialog among agencies and citizens. Open discussions about how to respond in such threatening circumstances as active shooters also promotes wise actions—including the heroic steps taken by the individuals described previously. Active shooter training, for example, is provided for employees and students at an increasing rate. This training invites individuals to join in the dialog about how to better secure the buildings where they work. Failing to engage in such partnership-forming dialog is a failure to embrace the tremendous potential for publics to contribute to their own protection.

Key Takeaways for Forming Partnerships With Publics

1) Publics do not panic in crisis situations and they are not a burden. Rather, publics have a rich potential for serving as productive partners for reducing risk and advancing crisis recovery.
2) The crucial purpose of engaged partnerships in a risk and crisis setting is never to simply benefit the organization. The goal is always promoting the safety and well-being of all publics served by the organization.
3) Partnerships require that communication operates as a transaction between organizations or government agencies and their publics.
4) Ideally, partnerships emerge as a product of dialog. In other words, both parties value the relationship, seek the best for the other parties, and are willing to adapt their policies and behaviors based on mutual respect for ideas shared and for the emotions experienced by all parties.
5) A single message to a mass audience, although potentially helpful as a warning, does not create dialog and engaged partnerships. Rather, messages tailored for and refined through interactions with subgroups, initiated by any of the parties involved, can foster the partnerships we advocate

References

Department of Homeland Security. (n.d.). If you see something, say something. Retrieved from https://www.dhs.gov/see-something-say-something/about-campaign

Getchell, M. C. (2017). Chaos, informational voids, and emergent organizations: The case of West Virginia's water and freedom industries. In C. J. Liberman, D. Rodriguez, & T. A. Avtgis (Eds.), *Casing crisis and risk communication* (pp. 1–8). Dubuque, IA: Kendall Hunt.

Green, S. J. (2016, October 11). Man who ended shooting at Seattle Pacific University takes stand in gunman's trial. *The Seattle Times.* Retrieved from http://www.seattletimes.com/seattle-news/crime/man-who-ended-shooting-at-seattle-pacific-university-takes-stand-in-gunmans-trial

Herovic, E., Sellnow, T. L., & Anthony, K. E. (2014). Risk communication as interacting arguments: Viewing the L'Aquila earthquake disaster through the message convergence framework. *Argumentation and Advocacy, 51,* 73–86.

Kent, M. L., & Lane, A. B. (2017). A rhizomatous metaphor for dialogic theory. *Public Relations Review, 43,* 568–578.

Kent, M. L., & Taylor, M. (1998). Building dialogic relationships through the world wide web. *Public Relations Review, 24*(3), 321–334.

Kent, M. L., & Theunissen, P. (2016). Elegy for mediated dialogue: Shiva the destroyer and reclaiming our first principles. *International Journal of Communication, 10,* 4040–4054.

Lane, A., & Kent, M. L. (2018). Dialogic engagement. In K. Johnson, & M. Taylor (Eds.), *Handbook of communication engagement* (pp. 61–72). Malden, MA: Wiley-Blackwell.

National Crime Prevention Council. (n.d.). Neighborhood Watch. Retrieved from https://www.ncpc.org/resources/home-neighborhood-safety/neighborhood-watch

National Research Council (1989). *Improving risk communication.* Washington, DC: National Academy Press.

Noar, S. M., Benac, C. N., & Harris, M. S. (2007). Does tailoring matter? Meta-analytic review of tailored print health behavior change interventions. *Psychological Bulletin, 133*(4), 673–693.

Passengers help stop possible terror attack on Detroit bound plane. (2009, December 26). *Fox News.* Retrieved from http://www.foxnews.com/story/2009/12/26/passengers-help-stop-possible-terror-attack-on-detroit-bound-plane.html

Reynolds, B., & Seeger, M. W. (2005). Crisis and emergency risk communication as an integrative model. *Journal of Health Communication, 10,* 43–55.

Rincon, M. (2017, September 8). Houston jumps in to volunteer. *Houston Chronicle*. Retrieved from http://www.chron.com/life/article/Houston-jumps-in-to-volunteer-12184262.php

Sheppard, B., Rubin, G. J., Wardman, J. K., & Wessely, S. (2006). Terrorism and dispelling the myth of a panic prone public. *Journal of Public Health Policy, 27*(3), 219–245.

Sellnow, T. L., & Sellnow, D. D. (2010). The instructional dynamic of risk and crisis communication: Distinguishing instructional messages from dialogue. *The Review of Communication, 10*(2), 111–125.

Sellnow, T. L., Sellnow, D. D., Lane, D. R., & Littlefield, R. S. (2012). The value of instructional communication in crisis situations: Restoring order to chaos. *Risk Analysis, 32*(4), 633–643.

Taylor, M., & Kent, M. L. (2014). Dialogic engagement: Clarifying foundational concepts. *Journal of Public Relations Research, 26*(5), 384–398.

Ulmer, R. R., Sellnow, T. L., & Seeger, M. W. (2015). *Effective crisis communication: Moving from crisis to opportunity* (3rd ed.). Thousand Oaks, CA: Sage.

5

Public Concern

Listen to and Acknowledge Concerns of Publics

To be open and to create effective partnerships, an organization experiencing or managing a risk or crisis must listen to the concerns of its publics, take these concerns into account, and respond accordingly. Whether accurate or not, the perception of publics is their reality. If publics believe a risk exists, they can be expected to act according to that belief. If they believe a crisis is severe, acknowledging and responding to this belief are essential. For example, accusations of restaurants causing food poisoning can be posted by customers and widely viewed on social media outlets such as Twitter or Facebook or on well-trafficked Internet sites such as iwaspoisoned.com (Arnold, 2017). In some cases, these posts are highly accurate. In fact, some state health agencies monitor Twitter posts or online searches related to food poisoning to identify emerging outbreaks. In many cases, however, restaurants are unfairly blamed by misinformed consumers who assume the cause of their digestive malady stems from their last meal or the last meal outside their own home. Consequently, restaurants may be unjustly accused of a problem they did not cause. The result can be a reputational crisis for the restaurant. In these cases, restaurants must provide a substantial response to an unsubstantiated but nevertheless potentially damaging accusation.

As this example clearly illustrates, simply telling publics they don't understand and should not be afraid when something bad is happening is not usually effective. Generally, a much more effective strategy is to begin by acknowledging the concern or fear and then providing information about what is being done and how the crisis or risk is being managed. Monitoring the opinions of publics about risk prior to a crisis and about perceived severity after a crisis is essential to treating them as partners. This information provides the basis for adapting messages to the dynamic needs of publics.

Communication in Times of Trouble: Best Practices for Crisis and Emergency Risk Communication, First Edition. Matthew W. Seeger and Timothy L. Sellnow.
© 2019 John Wiley & Sons, Inc. Published 2019 by John Wiley & Sons, Inc.

How Do Publics Respond to Risks?

Peter Sandman (2012) worked to alter the way communication practitioners view crisis with his plainspoken distinction between hazard and risk. Sandman explained these two terms are now used in combination by most organizations and agencies managing the issues associated with risks. Sandman further explained that hazard accounts for the science behind the risk. A hazard is the statistical likelihood of a particular subgroup being exposed to a given risk. The threshold for any risk to cause harm to a group is also a component of hazard. Conversely, outrage is the emotional reaction individuals have to a given risk. The fear of a given risk or the anger generated by those who feel they are unfairly or unnecessarily exposed to a risk are examples of outrage. Thus, risk must be viewed as more than just the statistical or scientific likelihood of exposure or harm. Rather, risk is a function of both hazard and risk. If organizations and crisis communication practitioners want to communicate effectively with publics about a given risk, they must account for both the hazard and the outrage generated by the risk (Lachlan & Spence, 2007; Sandman, 2012).

The challenge for practitioners is that many people are inconsistent or unpredictable in how or when they will acknowledge hazards or express their outrage. An individual may, for example, become fearful of flying after observing news coverage of an airplane crash but frequently drive without a seatbelt, which is a much more immediate hazard. A distressing but convincing example of this inconsistency occurred in June 2017 in Florida. A husband and wife pulled over on the side of the highway and died after overdosing on illegally obtained fentanyl, a powerful synthetic opioid. Although the two obviously did not heed constant warnings about the epidemic of opioid abuse and the urgent risk of death from overdose, they displayed signs of recognizing and responding to hazards for their children. As the couple died, their children were in the back seat, clean, fed, appropriately dressed, and sleeping while strapped safely in car seats, which is how they were found several hours after their parents died (Kassab, 2017).

What Communication Challenges Do Hazards Create?

The key challenge in communicating hazards to diverse publics resides in the unending need to translate technical information into messages that can be understood and comprehended by nonscientists. Failing to provide this translation creates an information void that often heightens outrage and a poor translation can leave audiences even more confused. Thus, scientists are faced with the task of explaining and justifying recommendations that are based on volumes of highly complex data and reasoning that requires specialized training to understand. If the translation is too simple, communicators run the risk of being accused by their peers in the scientific community of sending inaccurate or incomplete messages. If the translation remains too technical, communicators risk overwhelming or confusing publics.

This challenge in communicating hazards is plainly demonstrated in the example that begins this section. Foodborne illness in the United States is a serious problem. The Centers for Disease Control and Prevention (CDC) estimates that 48 million people experience foodborne illnesses and 3,000 die from food-related diseases and complications every year (Arnold, 2017). Although restaurants are to blame in some of these cases, the origin of the majority involve food prepared at home, not in restaurants. Agencies such as the Food and Drug Administration (FDA) sponsor ongoing public campaigns such as "Fight BAC!" to draw awareness to problems in food preparation and to provide advice on avoiding the spread of harmful bacteria in food preparation and storage. The Fight BAC! campaign uses cartoon illustrations, simplified lists of basic steps, and common examples to help people comprehend the complexities of food technology. Some steps are easier to understand than others. For example, emphasizing that raw meats should not be prepared on the same surface or with the same knife as raw fruits or vegetables unless the surface and utensil are thoroughly washed is doable for most people. Recommendations to use a meat thermometer in the preparation of hamburgers, roasts, turkeys, and other meats to ensure the center of the food has reached a high enough temperature to kill bacteria are more difficult. Many people do not have a meat thermometer and many others have difficulty comprehending how or where to insert such thermometers or how to read them. Long-held traditions in preparing and serving food may also run counter to the recommendations provided by the FDA. The way people define washed or clean may also differ. For some, a surface or a knife is clean when it is rinsed or wiped with the same rag or sponge used to clean other surfaces. Unfortunately, this can lead to harmful bacteria being spread to other foods. The challenges in translating hazards are equally difficult in matters of driver safety, sheltering in place, earthquake readiness and response, and fire safety. Publics mean well, but accuracy in comprehension and ability and willingness to follow through on advice provided in warnings from organizations and agencies varies.

Relying on numbers to communicate hazards also poses challenges. Numerical expressions, no matter how statistically significant, about the prevalence or lack of immediate risk are potentially no less puzzling or tedious for publics than words. The explanation for this disinterest in numerical representations of hazard involves two factors. First, some kinds of numerical representations are difficult to comprehend for many publics (Slovic, 2010). Second, numerical representations of risk often conflict with our intuitive assumptions. Although the difficulty of publics in comprehending numerical representations is well documented, the fact that most hazards are expressed in terms of probability poses an added challenge. Probabilities inherently draw attention to the fact that there is a chance, sometimes high and sometimes low, that the risk will not manifest. Think about the phrase "500-year flood." Does this mean a bad flood will happen only once every 500 years and, once a bad flood is over, everyone is safe for another 499 years? This kind of misunderstanding of probability invites chance taking. A 500-year flood actually means there is a 1 in 500 chance of a flood of great magnitude happening in any given year. We also express some risks in terms of percentages, suggesting, for example, that there is a 50% chance of a hurricane ever making landfall in a specific town. Percentages are also difficult for some people to grasp and may lead individuals to misinterpret the meaning of probability statements—in some cases, deriving the opposite understanding of the one intended.

Herovic (2016) explains that the objectivity provided by quantitative explanations of hazards is often trumped by the deep-seated opinions and assumptions of publics. These opinions are not easily changed because they routinely bring publics comfort in coping with, denying, or ignoring prevalent risks. These problems are based on the tendency for publics to think quickly and intuitively about hazards (Slovic, 2010). Fast, intuitive thinking does not afford people the time needed to carefully weigh evidence and determine the level of threat to them or their families. The potential for changing existing behaviors is greatly diminished by this disinterest in moving from a fast, intuitive thought process about hazards to a slow, evidence-based assessment.

These challenges certainly do not mean that communication campaigns designed to share the facts about hazards are pointless. Rather, careful translation of technical information that is revised based on feedback provided by publics through message testing can make a positive difference. Efforts such as Fight BAC! have changed how many Americans store, prepare, and eat food. As we discussed previously, the United States Geological Survey (USGS) sponsored campaigns, including the ShakeOut drill, to teach residents what to do during earthquakes, which has millions of people participating in drills annually. Warnings about hazards work very well when publics both understand the warnings and are willing and able to follow the advice. Therefore, translations will most likely be effective when agencies can boil their messages down to the most urgent facts that make the most sense in justifying a reasonable course of action. Risk communicators should evaluate their messages by testing them with their publics often (Venette, 2008). Many messages about hazards fail to produce the desired effects because they fail to personally connect the information with the intended audience. People need to know how the risk affects them and their families and see how their actions can reduce or eliminate the risk for their families. If messages do not, in the eyes of the receiver, warrant the prescribed actions, the messages are likely to fail in creating the desired response.

What Communication Challenges Does Outrage Create?

Publics express a wide range of emotions in their outrage about risks and crises. Some of these emotions are potentially helpful, others are not. Most important, risk and crisis communicators must understand the emotional states of the publics they address. Without this essential audience analysis, the likelihood of communicating successfully is greatly diminished. For example, explaining that genetically modified foods pose no appreciable risk will likely fail, regardless of the evidence available, if the audience is outraged by the thought of their normal food being replaced with genetically modified fruits, vegetables, and grains. To those outraged by genetically modified organisms (GMOs), these alterations are reminiscent of the horrors created in fictional accounts like the story of Frankenstein. A dramatic example of this reaction occurred in Zambia during a famine. The Zambian president turned away food offered by countries such as the United States because he did not want to expose the people of his country to GMOs. He argued that if European countries refused to eat such food, his people should not be asked to do so just because they are poor (Ratzan, 2002).

The International Food Information Council (IFIC, n.d.) understands the outrage generated by genetically modified foods. IFIC is a neutral, nonprofit organization whose goal is to share accurate information about food and nutrition to promote good nutrition worldwide. In an effort to respect the emotions and potential outrage of global publics concerned about GMOs, IFIC has traveled to countries large and small, rich and developing, and interacted directly with their government leaders and media representatives. IFIC's goal is to listen to the concerns shared by publics they meet and provide a balanced explanation of the science.

They frame the entire interaction in the context of food security—helping countries make decisions that help ensure their growing populations have safe and secure food supplies and that there will be enough nutritious food and clean water available. In this manner, IFIC accepts the existing outrage and frames the issue in the context of ensuring the world's growing population will have adequate food and water far into the future.

Research can help explain the failure in Zambia and the reasoning behind IFIC's efforts. Jin (2014) explains that emotional responses vary widely among publics and among issues. Those who are experiencing anger or frustration are more likely to remain in the stage of venting their anger and resisting the actions of those seen as responsible for the problem. Others who are less angry and more fearful respond to the stress generated by the issue with a sense of urgency to resolve the problem by seeking more information or taking steps to reduce the risk. Groups like IFIC seek to acknowledge the fear and anger generated by genetically modified foods, allow publics to express or vent their anger, and share resources that allow them to make their own decisions about how to address the risk. Without acknowledging this concern, well-meaning risk and crisis communicators are likely to intensify rather than resolve the problem. Jin describes this process as "maximizing mutual understanding and closing gaps" between affected publics' "coping strategies and organization's responses" (p. 98).

How Should Agencies and Organizations Acknowledge the Concerns of Publics?

As we explained in this section, organizations cannot address concern or outrage by overwhelming publics with scientifically sound and objective facts and reasoning. If publics believe those in power are doing too little to address a risk that outrages them, more evidence will likely be seen as an effort to further confuse an already complicated issue. Worse, if there is an element of disagreement among agencies and organizations, publics begin to see the issue as politicized and may step even further away from actively considering protective actions. The goal is to anticipate, acknowledge, and, only after these two steps are complete, respond to concerns of publics. For example, one of IFIC's goals in its public communication is to assist publics in matching their concerns about chemicals in foods with the actual risk levels determined by extensive scientific research. IFIC's messages consistently begin with acknowledging public concern based on their survey research. Only after acknowledging such concerns does IFIC introduce evidence and recommendations that support or conflict with consumer opinions and concerns.

How Do Organizations and Agencies Anticipate Which Issues Are Likely to Produce Public Outrage?

Overlooking potential public concern is common for agencies and organizations. Neglecting public opinion is not necessarily inspired by manipulation. Rather, publics do not attend to many of the risks that affect their daily lives. In fact, as Sandman (2012) explains, publics are often difficult to outrage. In the best cases, publics feel a general sense of trust that risk issues are being managed by those charged with regulation. In worse cases, those managing the risks are assumed to be disinterested and uncaring. Efforts by watchdog groups to create outrage are met with the same skepticism as efforts to dismiss a risk. How, then, can we anticipate which risks are likely to create outrage? The answer is a combination of analysis and listening.

Sandman (2012) suggests that answering 12 questions about a risk issue will help determine the potential for the issue to generate outrage:

1) Is it voluntary or coerced?
2) Is it natural or industrial?
3) Is it familiar or exotic?
4) Is it not memorable or memorable?
5) Is it not dreaded or dreaded?
6) Is it chronic or catastrophic?
7) Is it knowable or not knowable?
8) Is it controlled by them or by others?
9) Is it fair or unfair?
10) Is it morally irrelevant or morally relevant?
11) Can I trust you or not?
12) Is the process responsive? (p. 13)

If the issue is seen by publics as voluntary, natural, familiar, not memorable, not dreaded, chronic, knowable, controlled by them, fair, and morally irrelevant, severe outrage is unlikely. Similarly, if the agencies or organizations responsible for managing the risk are seen as trusted and responsive, the potential for outrage is diminished. As answers to any of these questions move in the opposite direction, however, the likelihood of outrage increases.

The dynamic nature of risk communication is also important to emphasize. An issue that generates no outrage today may move to the forefront of public consciousness and result in tremendous outrage tomorrow. For example, lean finely textured beef (LFTB) was used for decades as an ingredient in canned food products and ground hamburger. LFTB is fat-free beef extracted from bones using a heating and separation technique. When ABC News broadcasted what it called an investigative report depicting America's hamburger as adulterated by what is called "pink slime," consumers became outraged by the use of LFTB—an ingredient they had consumed for years. Because of public outrage, fast-food chains such as McDonald's and several large grocery store chains pledged to stop selling products containing pink slime/LFTB. One of the primary producers of LFTB, Beef Products Incorporated (BPI), faced severe financial losses because of this public outrage. The company sued ABC News, claiming false reporting caused losses of nearly $2 billion. The case went to trial, but before a verdict was reached, ABC News settled the case by agreeing to pay BPI what is assumed to be an extremely large sum of money (Taylor, 2017). Despite the outcome of the lawsuit, the ABC News story did considerable financial harm by creating outrage focused on an issue that had previously been ignored by consumers. Many other cases have occurred where the public has become outraged by faulty or misleading information.

How Can Organizations Communicate to Prevent and Manage Outrage?

Outrage can be effectively countered with well-designed messages based on a thorough understanding of the audience, the issue at hand, and the competing messages (Degeneffe, Kinsey, Stinson, & Ghosh, 2009). Ideally, agencies and organizations can anticipate potential problems or observe subtle warnings that outrage is beginning to develop with their publics. These observations can be part of the ongoing process of monitoring their communication environments. If a problem is anticipated, agencies and organizations can actually inoculate against outrage (Parker, Rains, & Ivanov, 2016). Inoculation in risk and crisis communication involves a process of sharing two-sided persuasive messages about key issues that concern them. The two-sided messages are presented in a way that, on one hand, acknowledges potential concerns, and, on the other hand, explains how these concerns have already been resolved. The goal is for the message describing resolution to be stronger than the message depicting concerns. In message design, "inoculation" is a metaphor for how the term is used in medicine. Inoculations against disease involve patients receiving a weakened dose of a virus. The body is able to overwhelm this weakened dose and create antibodies against future encounters with the disease, which is how diseases such as polio and measles were largely eradicated. Two-sided messages expose publics to potential concerns and then provide a degree of immunity by providing them with counterarguments they can rehearse in their minds, consciously or subconsciously. When these inoculated individuals are exposed to outrageous claims in the future, they are more likely to engage in counterarguments rather than succumb to the outrage. The inoculation process is doomed to fail, however, unless the messages are designed and distributed with the well-being and best interest of publics at heart. If an inoculation message is designed to manipulate publics with dishonest information or for personal gain, the messages themselves will contribute to public outrage.

Current research has shown that inoculation messages can reduce outrage against such government agencies as the Travel Security Administration (TSA). In a recent study, a national sample of individuals was divided into two groups: one received an inoculation message and the other did not (Ivanov et al., 2016). The inoculation messages presented a two-sided persuasive message explaining that although TSA faces a constant threat of attack against U.S. citizens, the agency has frequently thwarted such attempts. The message further stated that if such an attack were to succeed, TSA is prepared to respond immediately to restore safe travel and protect the public. Both groups were then led through a simulation of an attack on an airline passenger jet. In response to the scenario, both groups were understandably upset and lost a degree of their confidence in the United States to prevent such attacks. Those who received the inoculation message, however, lost less confidence and regained their confidence much more quickly than those in the group that did not receive the inoculation message (Ivanov et al., 2016). Those who received the inoculation message, however, were far less outraged and regained their confidence much more quickly than those who did not. Follow-up assessments found that those who received the inoculation by way of conversation with those who received the message directly may have also been inoculated against extreme feelings of outrage. Thus, inoculation messages may have a far-reaching impact on risk decision making. Other preliminary research has also shown the potential for inoculation to provide readers and viewers with the skill to identify falsely attributed (fake) news. Inoculation messages are a viable tool available to agencies and organizations that effectively monitor their environments and anticipate unwarranted public outrage.

Summary

Perception is reality for publics facing risks. Thus, organizations must comprehend these concerns and consistently acknowledge them in their crisis communication. Organizations listen to publics' concerns by recognizing a wide range of responses within the categories of hazard, outrage, and apathy. Considerable caution is needed in translating complex scientific research into recommendations for publics affected by a risk or crisis. Before developing communication campaigns or warning messages, organizations and agencies are advised to survey the opinions of publics and adapt as needed.

Key Takeaways for Acknowledging Public Concern

1) Whether accurate or not, the perception of publics is their reality. If publics believe a risk exists, they can be expected to act according to that belief. Thus, any crisis response must address the publics' concerns.

2) Messages must account for both hazard and outrage in responding to public concern. Hazard refers to the statistical likelihood of a particular subgroup being exposed to a given risk. Conversely, outrage is the emotional reaction, such as fear or anger, individuals have in reaction to a given risk.

3) The key challenge in communicating hazards to diverse publics resides in the unending need for translating technical information into messages that can be understood and comprehended by nonscientists. Effective translations can help publics comprehend their actual risk and thereby reduce feelings of outrage.

4) Numerical expressions about the prevalence or lack of immediate risk, no matter how statistically significant, often lack influence with publics. If publics believe those in power are doing too little to address a risk that outrages them, more evidence will likely be seen as an effort to further confuse an already complicated issue. Thus, audience analysis is essential to fully comprehend the actions needed to address public outrage.

5) If the issue is seen by publics as voluntary, natural, familiar, not memorable, not dreaded, chronic, knowable, controlled by them, fair, and morally irrelevant, severe outrage is unlikely. Similarly, if the agencies or organizations responsible for managing the risk are seen as trusted and responsive, the potential for outrage is diminished.

References

Arnold, K. (2017, August 8). Eateries fret over food-poison posts. *Orlando Sentinel*, pp. A1–A2.

Degeneffe, D., Kinsey, J., Stinson, T., & Ghosh, K. (2009). Segmenting consumers for food defense communication strategies. *International Journal of Physical Distribution & Logistics Management, 39*(5), 365–403.

Herovic, E. (2016). *The challenges of communicating low probability and high consequence risks: Recommendations for earthquake pre-crisis and emergency-risk communication.* Lexington, KY: University of Kentucky.

International Food Information Council Foundation. (n.d.). *Food Insight.* Retrieved from https://www.foodinsight.org/about

Ivanov, B., Burns, W. J., Sellnow, T. L., Petrun-Sayers, E. L., Veil, S. R., & Mayorga, M. W. (2016). Using an inoculation message approach to promote public confidence in protective agencies. *Journal of Applied Communication Research, 44,* 381–398.

Jin, Y. (2014). Examining publics' crisis responses according to different shades of anger and sympathy. *Journal of Public Relations Research, 26,* 79–101.

Kassab, B. (2017, June 9). Parents who were found dead along I-4 with kids in back seat overdosed on fentanyl. *Orlando Sentinel.* Retrieved from http://www.orlandosentinel.com/news/breaking-news/os-volusia-couple-fentanyl-overdose-20170609-story.html

Lachlan, K. A., & Spence, P. R. (2007). Hazard and outrage: Developing a psychometric instrument in the aftermath of Katrina. *Journal of Applied Communication Research, 35,* 109–123.

Parker, K. A., Rains, S. A., & Ivanov, B. (2016). Examining the "blanket of protection" conferred by inoculation: The effects of inoculation messages on the cross-protection of related attitudes. *Communication Monographs, 83,* 49–68.

Ratzan, S. C. (2002). Interpretations, actions, and implications of scientific progress. *Journal of Health Communication, 7,* 369–370 doi: 10.1080/10810730290001756

Sandman, P. (2012). *Responding to community outrage: Strategies for effective risk communication* (First published in 1993 by the American Industrial Hygiene Association. Copyright transferred to the author in 2012). Retrieved from http://psandman.com/media/RespondingtoCommunityOutrage.pdf

Slovic, P. (2010). *The feeling of risk: New perspectives on risk perception.* London, UK; Washington, DC: Earthscan: In association with the International Institute for Environment and Development.

Taylor, K. (2017, August 9). ABC settled "pink slime" lawsuit for $177 million, leaving the beef company feeling "vindicated." *Business Insider.* Retrieved from http://www.businessinsider.com/pink-slime-case-177-million-settlement-2017-8

Venette, S. J. (2008). Risk as an inherent element in the study of crisis communication. *Southern Communication Journal, 73*(3), 197–210 doi: 10.1080/10417940802219686

6

Honesty

Communication With Honesty, Frankness, and Openness

One of the most important best practices of effective crisis communication is to be honest and open. Honesty is usually described as a fundamental ethical standard for communicators. Honesty means telling the truth to the best of your ability as well as committing to finding the truth. Openness suggests a high level of transparency and means information is shared freely and in a way that is understandable to stakeholders. Openness also means that leaders and spokespersons are accessible to their stakeholders and communicate with them. In practice, honesty and openness work together and are very closely associated. Effective crisis communicators are honest and open in their public communications.

As noted earlier, honesty is necessary to build the credibility of both crisis communicators and crisis messages. Being honest and open about risks helps people know what to do when a crisis hits. In addition, if information about a crisis is not shared openly by the organization engaged in the crisis, publics will obtain information from other sources (Spence & Lachlan, 2016). These alternative sources may be hostile and sometimes their messages are inaccurate—this is another way the organization can lose its ability to manage the crisis message(s) successfully. If an organization wishes to have its side of the story told during a crisis, it must be open. In addition, honesty is just the right way to approach our ethical obligations as crisis communicators. Such honesty, in the long run, creates credibility and trust with both the media and publics. A response that is less than honest may actually enhance the perception that the organization is doing something wrong and trying to cover it up.

Communication in Times of Trouble: Best Practices for Crisis and Emergency Risk Communication, First Edition. Matthew W. Seeger and Timothy L. Sellnow.
© 2019 John Wiley & Sons, Inc. Published 2019 by John Wiley & Sons, Inc.

Why Is It So Important to Be Honest?

Honesty has been described as a fundamental standard for ethical communication (Johannesen, Valde, & Whedbee, 2008). By that we mean honesty is one of the most basic ways whereby we describe communication as good or bad, right or wrong, desirable or undesirable. Lying is generally considered bad and wrong. Honesty is good and desirable for several reasons. First, if people were not essentially honest with one another, there would be no trust. Trust is an expectation that people and organizations will keep their word, act responsibly, meet their obligations, and follow basic social norms and rules. Without trust, people simply cannot work together. We have to trust that people are honest and telling us the truth when we interact with them. Without some basic trust in our organizations we would be much less willing to work with them or buy their products. Cooperation is based on a sense of trust and believing that other people are going to do what they say they will do. What would it be like if you assumed that others you worked with on projects, or interacted with daily, were always lying? What would it be like if you assumed that every message you received from an organization, a hospital, food company, university, or technology firm was a lie? It would be almost impossible to interact with those organizations or to accomplish tasks.

Second, we need people and organizations to be honest with us so we can make informed choices and decisions. Senders who are dishonest in the information they are communicating deny others the ability to make correct decisions. The ability to receive and evaluate information and use it to make choices and decisions is an important part of being human. People also have the right to make their own decisions. Telling people that contaminated water is safe to drink means that they will likely make choices that can harm them or their family. Deciding not to report defective ignition switches or faulty tires means people will be denied information about how to protect themselves and their families. Withholding information that a food item may be contaminated with *Salmonella* bacteria denies people the ability to protect themselves and their families. Being honest with others is a way to show respect for their ability to make rational and informed decisions. This may be especially hard, however, when the information is about a risky situation or a crisis when all the information about the risks simply is not available. In addition, being honest may mean communicating information that reflects negatively on the organization. Mary Barra, chief executive officer (CEO) of General Motors (GM), publicly acknowledged the company had withheld information about faulty ignition switches on GM cars. In this case, admitting the company had been dishonest may have increased legal liability but it was the right thing to do.

Finally, honesty is important to building and sustaining strong relationships. When organizations are open and honest with their customers, they build trust and create strong connections and brand loyalty. When organizations are open and honest with their suppliers, they create more stable and effective networks and supply chains. Honesty can become a very important part of an organization's reputation and loyalty is a very valuable resource. Trust in a company brand can be an economic asset to an organization. Organizations can build on this resource and create a reservoir of goodwill by being honest and open with their stakeholders. This resource of goodwill can be critical during a crisis. Good will can translate directly into support from stakeholders including customers and suppliers. There are many cases where an organization was able to successfully manage a crisis because it had a very positive reputation.

One of the most famous cases of product tampering occurred in 1982. Packages of the over-the-counter painkiller Tylenol were intentionally contaminated. The deadly poison cyanide was added to the capsules, which were returned to the stores and put back on the shelves. Customers bought the contaminated capsules and seven people died from the poisoning. The parent company, Johnson and Johnson, responded very quickly to recall any unsold packages, issued warnings to publics, and rapidly redesigned their packages so they were triple sealed and tamper proof. By taking these actions, the company protected the brand image and sales of their product quickly rebounded. Customers trusted that the company had been honest and done the right thing. The CEO went on national television to say that, based on the evidence, the tampering occurred at the retail stores, but he did not attempt to shift blame. Being honest and open in this case helped protect the brand and helped the company recover quickly from what could have been a devastating crisis.

Can you imagine a case where a company intentionally withheld information about the risks of using their products? Do organizations make claims about their products and services that are false or misleading? Would you say most people trust the messages that organizations communicate? Unfortunately, withholding information and deceptive advertising are very common. This is one of the major reasons many people distrust large corporations. Financial services organizations, oil companies, Internet service providers, government agencies, pharmaceutical companies, and health insurance providers are just some of the industries that typically rank very low in terms of reputation. As a consequence, organizations in these industries will have a more difficult time managing a crisis successfully than organizations with reputations for being honest and trustworthy.

Another more recent case shows the consequences of being dishonest. On September 18, 2015, the United States Environmental Protection Agency (EPA) issued a notice of violation of the U.S. Clean Air Act to the German automaker Volkswagen (VW) Group. This was based on information that the company had intentionally programmed its diesel engines to activate certain emissions controls only during laboratory emissions tests. This software essentially allowed the cars to avoid the emissions tests that were required for cars to be sold in the United States. The software allowed VW cars to emit up to 40 times the allowable levels of U.S. emissions. The software was used in VW cars sold throughout the world. It is estimated around 11 million cars in at least 17 countries in Europe, North America, and Asia had this deceptive software. The resale value of these vehicles dropped significantly by an average of over $2,000 per car. Sales of new VW cars also dropped by about 15%. Some estimates place the cost to the company at $18 billion in legal fees, lost business, and fines. In addition, there will be a cost to public health as people suffer the health impacts of additional air pollution. Dishonesty and, in this case, deception had a very direct cost to the company and to the publics.

What Does It Really Mean to Be Honest?

Although honesty may seem like a very simple idea, it is not always straightforward or easy, especially during a crisis. Most of us think of honesty as just telling the truth. There are many cases where what is true just is not known, where there are multiple "truths," or where telling the truth could actually create more harm. During many crises, information is not adequate or available and people simply do not have the answers about what is happening, what might happen, or why it happened. This is a form of uncertainty, which almost always surrounds a crisis and is especially present during the earliest stages.

Being honest means being as truthful as possible given the specific situation. Some situations make it hard to be completely honest and open. As we have described before, crises are high uncertainty events. There is often much confusion about what is happening and sometimes investigating commissions, groups, or committees are used to sort out what caused a crisis. In the case of U.S. airline disasters, for example, the National Transportation and Safety Board (NTSB) conducts inquiries and makes recommendations for improvements in airline safety. These usually involve very detailed and complete investigations of technical failures, human error, environmental factors, and related issues that may have contributed to the accident. These investigations also include public hearings that enhance the openness of the investigation process. Since its founding, the NTSB has investigated more than 132,000 aviation accidents and issued over 13,000 safety recommendations.

Honesty is sometimes complicated by the need to respond very quickly. As we have discussed elsewhere, responding quickly to a crisis is important. Organizations often feel the need to communicate as quickly as possible and they try to reduce all of the confusion and uncertainty people might be feeling. Sometimes, this results in overreassurance. Although these impulses are generally positive, they can sometimes backfire when all the information eventually becomes clear. Many organizations have been forced to take back messages and retract statements when they find that their initial statements were overly optimistic. This is another way an organization can lose its ability to manage the crisis message successfully.

In a well-known case from 2006, 13 miners were trapped in the Sago coal mine in West Virginia. During the rescue, mining officials reported incorrectly that 12 of the survivors had been found alive; in fact, only one miner had actually survived. The initial message from the mine was misheard and communicated before it could be confirmed. The initial report gave false hope to the families who were later devastated when the real news came out. In many crises, the scope of the harm—how much oil has been spilled, how many people are sick, how much food has been contaminated, or how many social security numbers have been leaked—is simply not immediately known. How can organizations be honest when they do not have the information?

One answer is to simply acknowledge the uncertainty of the situation. We call this strategic ambiguity because it is a way to reflect the ambiguity and uncertainty of the crisis circumstance in the crisis message (Ulmer & Sellnow, 1997). If it is actually the case that the information is not known, it is appropriate to say, "We don't know exactly what is happening, but this is what we are doing to find out, and this is when we expect to have that information." This is an honest response and can help improve and preserve credibility. In some cases, organizations facing a crisis make claims about things that obviously cannot be known. During the Exxon Valdez oil spill, executives initially said the spill was very small, was well contained, and did not affect wildlife. It was clear, however, that at such an early stage in the crisis the impact of the spill simply could not be known. We further discuss uncertainty and how it is best managed in a later section.

As a crisis develops and more information becomes available, it may also be the case that earlier statements about what happened are clearly no longer correct. What should organizations say in those circumstances? First, organizations should be willing to be equivocal, especially early in the development of a crisis. Statements such as "based on what we currently know, this is what we believe" allow room for changes later when more is known. Second, if the understanding of a crisis situation does change, managers should acknowledge that earlier statements were incorrect.

In fall 2015, dozens of customers in California, Minnesota, New York, Ohio, Oregon, and Washington were sickened with a strain of Shiga toxin-producing *Escherichia coli* O26 (STEC O26). The outbreak was quickly traced to infected meat products distributed by the franchise restaurant Chipotle Mexican Grill. The Chipotle organization responded quickly to the incident, shutting down over 43 restaurants across the infected area and working closely with both the Food and Drug Administration (FDA) and the Centers for Disease Control and Prevention (CDC) to track down the source of the outbreak. Chipotle's quick response was followed by claims the crisis was over and the food was now safe. Subsequent outbreaks continued and in December 2015 some 80 college students in Boston were sickened after eating at a single Chipotle restaurant. The continued outbreaks even after the company claimed the crisis was over further undermined Chipotle's reputation and credibility and eroded its brand.

What Are Some Challenges to Being Honest During a Crisis?

As we described earlier, a number of impediments to honesty and openness exist during a crisis. Some of these impediments are structural, such as the fact that crises are almost always high uncertainty events, where information is often not immediately available. A primary challenge is the fact that we sometimes simply do not know what is happening, which makes it hard to be open and honest. In these cases, it is best to acknowledge that the facts are not yet known, share what is being done to get the information, and indicate when the information might be available. It is also important for organizations to do everything they can to get the information as quickly as possible so they can be open and honest.

Some impediments are perceptual, such as the myth of panic we discussed earlier, and the resulting tendency of public officials to withhold information. The myth of panic is the belief that if publics are told what is really happening, they will panic and do irrational and destructive things. The example often given is that people evacuated from a fire will run back into the burning building. People sometimes do run back into burning buildings, usually to recover something of value, such as pets or records, or to help others who may be trapped inside. This is more a case of impulsive behavior or poor decision making than panic. Panic is generally described as a sudden unreasoning and irrational terror often accompanied by thoughtless and erratic behaviors. Most people act in very logical and rational ways during a crisis. People may make decisions very quickly, often without much information, but actual panic during a crisis is very rare.

Organizations, however, often use the myth of panic as a justification for withholding information or issuing deceptive statements. Some chemical manufacturers have suggested that the general public simply is not capable of understanding how chemicals are processed and there will be irrational fear and panic if they know chemicals are being produced close to them. As a consequence, these companies argue they should not have to disclose information about their manufacturing processes. In these and many similar cases, the myth of panic is used as an excuse for withholding important information from publics. As we discussed previously, publics can experience a high degree of outrage when they feel a risk is unfairly being imposed on them or when information about a risk is being withheld. A better approach is to take the time to explain the risks in a clear and understandable manner and to work to build a genuine dialog so concerns can be heard and acted on.

In addition, crisis managers and organizations do not want to look uninformed so they may simply choose not to communicate or may overstate what they actually know about a crisis. During a crisis, managers may try to create the appearance they are in control and have all the facts and quick answers. Sometimes this involves overstating what is known and downplaying the harm or potential harm caused by a crisis.

Finally, many organizations have a clearance process for releasing information about a crisis. This process may require several people in the organization to review messages before they can be communicated. Top management, the legal department, various operational departments, and the public relations department sometimes have to review and approve any statement before it is communicated. Clearance processes can slow down the release of information and can result in messages that are less forthright and open.

Maintaining honesty and openness in spite of these challenges is a fundamental requirement of almost all crisis communication. Some impediments are political, such as when attorneys try to limit what is being said. Some impediments are structural, such as the uncertainty that surrounds a crisis and a clearance processes that can slow and change a message. Some are psychological, such as when managers are simply afraid to speak out. In a very few cases, openness may create more risks, such as in an ongoing active shooter crisis. Being honest and open is difficult during a crisis but is very important.

Sometimes, an organization has done something wrong and is thereby responsible for a crisis and for harming people. In these cases, there will be a great deal of pressure to avoid admitting any wrongdoing. Being honest does not necessarily require a full public confession of wrongdoing, but it does mean the organization should acknowledge its mistakes. In the long run, honestly acknowledging mistakes is a much more effective option than trying to hide them. Trying to hide mistakes in most cases adds an additional layer of harm to the crisis.

How Is Openness Achieved During a Crisis?

Whereas honesty means a commitment to finding and telling the truth, openness means making information accessible. Information should be in a form people can understand and distributed in ways that are accessible. Organizational spokespersons and leaders should be responsive. Openness is the opposite of secrecy and suggests some level of transparency and free access to information. Openness is also associated with collaboration and cooperation during a crisis. We have already pointed out that crises are high uncertainty events and that the facts are not always immediately available. Crises can also be very complex, with multiple factors interacting in unexpected ways. As we discussed previously and expand on in a later chapter, communicating highly technical information about a crisis in an understandable way can be very challenging. In some cases, the technical issues may make it hard to be open. For example, communicating accurately with publics about issues such as the impact of chemical exposure on public health or how food has been genetically modified is difficult. Nevertheless, it is very important in building and maintaining partnerships and true dialog with publics.

In other cases, those harmed in a crisis may be outraged and managers and spokespersons may not want to face angry questions and accusations. In these cases, managers may believe that avoiding any public appearance is the easiest and safest approach. This failure to be accessible may create the impression the company is trying to hide something. Sometimes, those affected by a crisis will confront the company CEO and managers. They may do so in public meetings, which could also include shareholder meetings. These encounters can be emotional and uncomfortable and it takes skill and patience to manage them. As we discussed earlier, people may feel outrage as a consequence of a crisis and want to express that. Part of the communication with publics about the water contamination in Flint, Mich., involved public meetings where officials tried to answer questions about what happened and why. Many of these meetings became very angry and confrontational, but the officials continued trying to answer questions in a calm and logical way while also acknowledging the anger. Their answers did not resolve the anger but they did promote openness.

Finally, as we have pointed out several times, there can be conflicts between the legal department and the public relations department over openness. During a crisis, attorneys are often very reluctant to say anything that may potentially increase legal liability. In some cases, they may even advise CEOs not to apologize following a crisis. Sadly, some studies have found that legal strategies tend to dominate during an organizational crisis (Fitzpatrick & Rubin, 1995). Failure to adopt a strategy of openness can be shortsighted and costly and compound the damage to an organization's reputation. In the case of United Airlines and the crisis created by forcibly removing a passenger from an overbooked flight, the CEO was slow to respond and apologize. Although it is not clear if a legal strategy was part of the decision to respond this way, part of the initial response defended the company based on the legal right to remove passengers. A cell phone video of a bloodied United Airlines passenger being dragged from the plane went viral and created an intense crisis for the company. Regardless of the legal right to remove passengers, the very negative publicity from the crisis harmed the company.

The perspective of attorneys and legal departments is not necessarily wrong. Rather, it is just one side of the strategy for responding to a crisis. Another side is the public relations and crisis communication perspective. In the best cases, public relations and legal are both represented in the discussion about how to be open and transparent during a crisis. This openness, as we discuss next, can be aided by social media.

Social media can help an organization be open and honest by creating a capacity to communicate information quickly and very broadly. Company Twitter accounts can be used to quickly communicate about developments in crisis. The CEO of United Airlines used Twitter to announce changes to company policy following its violent removal of a passenger. YouTube can also be very effective for communicating statements from the CEO, including explanations and, in some cases, apologies. The CEO of Maple Leaf Foods used YouTube to apologize for a 2008 outbreak of listeria associated with their meat products, which was linked to 22 deaths. Social media can also help organizations learn what information publics are seeking. This knowledge can help organizations meet those information needs in an open and honest way (Lin, Spence, Sellnow, & Lachlan, 2016). Although social media can create problems when rumors and inaccurate information are spread, if it is managed correctly, social media can be helpful in promoting openness during a crisis. Social media is a very important tool for crisis communication and can play a central role in promoting honesty and openness, responding quickly, and getting feedback about how messages are being received.

Summary

Being honest and maintaining openness during a crisis are very challenging best practices. Honesty means telling the truth and committing to finding the truth. Openness means sharing information freely, even when that information may not reflect positively on the organization. Honesty and openness work together and support one another. Being open and honest requires a strong commitment by top management, often in the face of legal constraints, angry stakeholders, and lack of complete information. Throughout a crisis, communicators should ask themselves, "Are we being open about what is happening?" and "Are we being honest in what we are communicating?" Demonstrating openness and honesty builds credibility and can help protect an organization's image and brand.

Key Takeaways for Honesty and Openness

1) Honesty means telling the truth to the best of your ability as well as committing to finding the truth. Openness suggests a high level of transparency and means information is shared freely and in a way that is understandable to stakeholders. Being honest and open during a crisis is not always easy because information isn't always available and the conditions of a crisis may make it hard to be open with the information.

2) Honesty and openness are both associated with credibility. Credibility is an assessment that a communicator has expertise and is trustworthy. When messages come from credible sources, they are more likely to be believed and acted upon.

3) Honesty and openness can also help build a positive organizational reputation and build a reservoir of goodwill. This may mean stakeholders are more likely to help an organization during a crisis.

4) When information is not yet known or confirmed, the most honest response is to be equivocal about what is known and unknown. Statements like "based on what we currently know, this is what we believe" can help organizations be truthful even when facing uncertainty.

5) Honesty and openness are not only the most effective ways to communicate during a crisis, they are also fundamental ethics for communication. They are responsible ways to fulfill obligations for communicating during a crisis.

References

Fitzpatrick, K. R., & Rubin, M. S. (1995). Public relations vs. legal strategies in organizational crisis decisions. *Public Relations Review, 21*(1), 21–33.

Johannesen, R. L., Valde, K. S., & Whedbee, K. E. (2008). *Ethics in human communication.* Prospect Heights, IL: Waveland Press.

Lin, X., Spence, P. R., Sellnow, T. L., & Lachlan, K. A. (2016). Crisis communication, learning and responding: Best practices in social media. *Computers in Human Behavior, 65*, 601–605.

Spence, P. R., & Lachlan, K. A. (2016). Reoccurring challenges and emerging threats: Crises and the new millennium. In A. Schwarz, M. W. Seeger, & C. Auer (Eds.), *The handbook of international crisis communication research* (pp. 212–223). West Sussex, UK: Wiley.

Ulmer, R. R., & Sellnow, T. L. (1997). Strategic ambiguity and the ethic of significant choice in the tobacco industry's crisis communication. *Communication Studies, 48*(3), 215–233.

7

Collaboration

Collaborate and Coordinate With Credible Sources

In almost all cases, crises are abnormal events that require people, groups, companies, agencies, and communities to behave in nonroutine ways. Often this includes the participation and help of outside groups and stakeholders in responding to the crisis. Sometimes these are groups the organization facing a crisis knows well, such as suppliers and customers. In other cases, these may be groups the company has little experience with, such as regulatory agencies, government groups, first responders, and community support agencies. The support and cooperation of those groups and agencies can be very important in helping an organization successfully manage a crisis. Collaborating, coordinating, and cooperating with these groups is a best practice of crisis communication.

Good risk and crisis communication is based on establishing strategic partnerships with key groups and communities before a crisis occurs and maintaining those partnerships as the crisis develops. These collaborative relationships allow agencies and organizations to coordinate their plans, messages, and activities and pool their resources. Developing a precrisis network is a very effective way of coordinating and collaborating with other credible sources. To maintain effective networks, crisis planners and communicators should continuously seek to identify and validate sources of information, identify subject matter experts, and develop relationships with stakeholders at various levels. Coordinating messages enhances the probability of consistent content and may reduce the confusion the public experiences during a crisis. Consistency of messages between various stakeholders is one important benchmark of effective crisis communication.

Communication in Times of Trouble: Best Practices for Crisis and Emergency Risk Communication, First Edition. Matthew W. Seeger and Timothy L. Sellnow.
© 2019 John Wiley & Sons, Inc. Published 2019 by John Wiley & Sons, Inc.

Who Are the Credible Partners for an Organization?

All organizations have networks of stakeholders that they depend on and that depend on the organization. This may include customers, suppliers, community groups, stockholders and owners, governments, creditors, professional and trade associations, unions, and employees. Generally, these stakeholders are sources of support and resources for organizations and, during a crisis, can help out, especially if the organization has cultivated positive relationships and developed a reservoir of goodwill with them (Jones, Jones, & Little, 2000). As we discussed earlier, a positive reputation represents an important asset that an organization can invest in over time. This can translate into a powerful basis of support during a crisis. Those organizations with positive reputations are likely to weather a crisis much more successfully than those with negative reputations. Goodwill not only means that organizations may receive support from their stakeholders, it also means the messages these organizations communicate are more likely to be believed, accepted, and followed.

Credibility generally has two elements: trustworthiness and expertise. Trustworthiness involves honesty, transparency, and a general expectation that people will act in responsible ways and in the best interest of others. Expertise refers to some level of specialized knowledge, capacity, or skill. We are more likely to believe people when we think they are trustworthy and when they have expert knowledge. Identifying credible partners who can help out during a crisis will also depend on the specific organization and type of risks or crises they face. For example, a school system may want to coordinate its crisis plans with the state school boards, establish agreements with neighboring schools, and work with parent–teacher organizations. In the case of a crisis involving a food company, relationships with the public health community, as well as state and federal regulatory agencies such as the U.S. Food and Drug Administration, can be very important. Large transportation organizations, including airlines and trucking and shipping companies, should work to develop relationships with the National Highway Traffic Safety Administration (NHTSA). In almost all cases, industry trade associations, such as the International Food Information Council (IFIC) or the National Air Transportation Association (NATA), can serve as important resources for organizations. They can help show an organization is operating in a way that is consistent with standardized industry practice and can serve as a source of support during a crisis. Trade associations are generally credible partners and can serve as intermediaries in strategic communication activities before and during a crisis by providing additional resources and coordinating messages (Frandsen & Johansen, 2015).

Credible partners are those groups and agencies with a stake in the organization that can help spread messages and add legitimacy. For example, the Centers for Disease Control and Prevention (CDC) is a very well-respected and credible scientific and public health organization. Organizations that coordinate with the CDC around issues of infectious disease, injury prevention, or foodborne illness can boost their own credibility. This will make messages more effective. In the same way, investigations by the National Transportation Safety Board (NTSB) can help lend credibility to efforts to find out what happened in transportation accidents. Both the CDC and the NTSB are independent agencies, which means they do not have specific interests or agendas that can reduce their credibility.

In other cases, credible organizations are those that can bring specialized technical expertise. When Flint, Mich., faced a deadly outbreak of Legionnaires' disease following the decision to change its water supply, city officials contracted with a research university to investigate any possible connection between the water and the disease. Legionnaires' disease can occur when people inhale water that is contaminated with bacteria. The university researchers had the necessary technical expertise to investigate and were independent, meaning there were no conflicts of interest. Technical expertise is very helpful and organizations often look to university experts for help during a crisis.

Other credible partners during a crisis can be found in the communities that are affected by the crisis. People in the community can bring a kind of cultural expertise to a crisis (Quarantelli, 1982). Crises commonly affect some groups more so than others. For example, poorer people, minorities, people with disabilities, and members of immigrant communities are often hit hardest by crises (Spence & Lachlan, 2016). Often, these groups simply do not have the resources to prepare for or recover from a crisis. Reaching these communities with crisis messages can be improved if the organization uses representatives from those communities as liaisons. These representatives are sometimes called cultural agents and they may be community leaders, religious leaders, or leaders of cultural groups. Sometimes they are informal leaders. These leaders often have more credibility with their communities than outsiders. They usually are able to speak to members of the community using more familiar language and they understand the values and history of the community.

When considering which groups and individuals might make credible and supportive partners, it is important to choose carefully. Some partners can be controversial and can create additional problems or distractions when trying to manage the crisis. For example, many groups and organizations contributed bottled water to Flint, Mich. One organization was the water company Nestle. Nestle has water bottling plants in Michigan and was trying to win approval to triple the amount of water it was allowed to withdraw for its bottling operations. Some critics accused Nestle of using the Flint water crisis to further its own financial agenda. The controversy over Nestle distracted attention from the efforts to manage the Flint crisis and help the community.

A final stakeholder to keep in mind during a crisis is the media. Traditional media, especially those associated with journalism, will report on crises and will work to get the word out about what is happening, who is at risk, and what should be done. Organizations will have to depend on the media to spread important messages. In this way, the media serves as an important channel for crisis communication. During the 2017 California wildfires, the media played a critical role in updating the public on risks, evacuation routes, and shelters. They even helped companies inform employees about fire-related closures. In many cases, traditional media organizations also used social media to help update the public. Systems like interactive social media and maps were very important in helping track the California fires.

Sometimes, however, journalists trying to tell the story of a crisis can be aggressive and even confrontational. This is especially the case when they believe that important information is being withheld. During a crisis, journalists have an important role in getting the word out and telling the story of what happened and why. Being open and transparent with media organizations during a crisis is especially important, as we describe in a later chapter. Building relationships with the media before a crisis happens is one way to create more productive and open cooperation during a crisis. Some organizations even invite reporters to tour their facilities and observe their crisis exercises as a way to promote understanding and cooperation.

What Do Collaboration and Coordination Mean?

Collaboration means working with others to achieve some outcome. Collaborating suggests a close working relationship, such as in a partnership or team working to complete an important task. Many organizations have collaborative relationships with groups of stakeholders, such as customers, dealers, suppliers, or community groups. These relationships are usually mutually beneficial and generally built around mutual interdependence and dialog. Automotive dealers, for example, depend on the auto companies to produce high-quality products people want to buy and to market those products. The auto companies depend on dealers to sell and service products and to have a presence in the local community. In some cases, relationships between suppliers, companies, and dealers have lasted for decades. These relationships can be very helpful in sustaining an organization during a crisis.

From a public relations perspective, collaboration often means a two-way symmetrical relationship between an organization and its stakeholders (Grunig, 2001). This model of public relations is based on mutuality and equity and is designed as a way to create trust and mutual understanding between parties. When organizations and their stakeholders both communicate openly and honestly, they can develop a much clearer understanding of one another. As we discussed previously, this is sometimes described using the concept of a dialog for an open exchange of ideas, information, and perspectives. Trust between organizations and their stakeholders can help streamline collaboration before and during a crisis. Strong collaborative relationships can also help an organization avoid a crisis by helping the organization recognize warning signs before they become a crisis.

Coordination is somewhat different than collaboration. Coordination involves unifying activities to create a common outcome. This does not necessarily require working closely as a team and, in fact, it is possible to coordinate without even interacting directly with others. These unified activities may be very different, but they are integrated and synchronized in ways that contribute to a larger goal. One of the biggest problems in many crises is creating a coordinated response so all the parts of a response are working together. Coordination is often built around different areas of expertise. For example, during a crisis, expertise may be required to investigate what happened, stabilize the situation, locate and assist victims, and communicate what is being done. Different skills, capacities, and resources are often required to help manage a crisis and these will not necessarily be found in the organization. When schools face a crisis, for example, they may have to evacuate all the students. They will need large buildings to accommodate students. Other schools, churches, or even sports facilities can be used for these evacuations and having these plans and agreements in place in advance can be very important. In the case of contaminated food items, companies often have to coordinate with media outlets, regulators, distributors, wholesalers, and retail outlets. This kind of coordination requires everyone to understand their roles as well as what others will be doing.

Sometimes, coordination is built around various locations or regions. For example, evacuations may move people to several different shelters; creating a complete list of everyone who has been evacuated will require these locations to communicate with each other or with a third party. Some crises involve multiple regions or even multiple countries. In these cases, regional offices may need to coordinate their messages and activities with a central office. The 2017 California wildfires affected several counties and communities and evacuees were scattered around several shelters. Getting accurate information was necessary to determine the number of fatalities. As these examples show, coordination is usually created by communication or at least by sharing information about what others are doing. Well-designed networks for communicating during a crisis can make coordination much more successful. Contact lists with e-mail addresses and phone numbers as well as crisis plans can also help with coordination.

Finally, conducting crisis drills and tabletop exercises can help build collaborative relationships and facilitate coordination. Many people have participated in fire drills or tornado drills. Sadly, most schools now have so-called active shooter training where students prepare for the possibility of a mass shooting threat. These activities help people understand what they should do in a crisis situation and familiarize them with evacuation routes or shelter procedures. Tabletop exercises, according to the Federal Emergency Management Agency (FEMA; 2016), are discussion exercises of various issues regarding a hypothetical crisis situation. More specifically, FEMA (2016) states, "Tabletop exercises can be used to assess plans, policies, and procedures or to assess types of systems needed to guide the *prevention* of, *response* to, or *recovery* from a defined incident" (n.p.). As we described earlier, tabletop exercises usually bring together the people who would need to manage a crisis to discuss what they would do when facing a specific kind of emergency.

In addition to clarifying roles, responsibilities, and procedures, tabletops can help organizations identify weaknesses and gaps. One tabletop exercise we participated in uncovered a major flaw—the established procedures for a fire did not include notification of the facilities department. Tabletops can also clarify relationships. In another series of tabletop exercises between stakeholders involved in a public health crisis, we observed extensive arguments about who was actually going to be in control of the response. Obviously, it was better to have this argument during an exercise rather than during a real crisis event.

In many ways, collaboration and coordination simply mean working together to plan for, avoid, manage, or recover from a crisis. It is very difficult, although not impossible, to establish these kinds of relationships during an actual crisis, so it is a best practice to develop these partnerships before the crisis begins. These relationships are almost always necessary for the effective management of a crisis.

Why Are Collaboration and Coordination So Important?

As we discussed, a crisis is usually a confusing and sometimes chaotic time when people just do not know what is happening. This often translates into very uncoordinated and ineffective responses where people are given conflicting information and where responses are delayed. Coordination and communication with others are almost always necessary when mounting an effective crisis response. A number of case studies have shown breakdowns in communication and coordination during a crisis response. Among these are the breakdowns in communication between firefighters, police, and other emergency personnel following the World Trade Center disaster and the contradictory messages offered by government agencies during the 2014 Ebola pandemic in West Africa. In the case of the World Trade Center, the various emergency response agencies—the New York police, the fire department, and Port Authority officials—did not have radio systems that easily communicated with each other. This meant some responders did not get the evacuation orders and were caught in the tower when it collapsed. One of the recommendations coming out of the World Trade Center disaster was the creation of interoperable systems. This simply means the systems should allow people to communicate with one another even though they are working with different agencies. It is an important principle regardless of the crisis situation. In the case of the 2014 Ebola outbreak, a number of contradictory statements were made about how the disease was spread and who was at risk. Some of this information occurred through social media and was spread in part because experts were not fully engaged in communicating the risk. This resulted in confusion and wasted time and money. As these cases show, breakdowns in coordination can make a response less effective and might even create more harm, including lost lives.

In addition, most organizations simply do not have all the resources and specialized expertise to manage crises. They will need help. Sometimes this takes the form of information. Disease outbreaks, natural disasters, toxic spills, and many other kinds of crises require technical expertise to manage the risk and reduce harm. Sometimes help means additional personnel or even equipment. During many crises, the organization's public relations department will be overwhelmed with calls, requests for information, and inquiries from the media. Organizations need some ability to surge their capacity to communicate during a crisis and this can be provided by their external public relations agency or by mutual aid agreements with other organizations. In other cases, specialized skills are needed. After a case of workplace violence, employees may need psychological counseling. These services can often be provided by the organization's health insurance provider.

How Can an Organization Create Collaboration and Coordination?

As we described earlier, it's best to develop collaborative and cooperative relationships before a crisis occurs. In many ways, these kinds of relationships are not just a best practice of crisis communication, they are good public relations and just good management. An organization can start developing these relationships by first making a list of stakeholders and determining what credible partners might be needed during a crisis. Once these groups are identified, it is helpful to find out more about them, their goals, and capabilities.

Activities such as exercises and tabletops can help build collaboration and cooperation. Sharing information about crisis plans can also help create partnerships and promote coordination. Mutual training activities are also helpful in creating networks of support. If partners know about and understand the plan, they will have a better idea of what they should do during a crisis. Plans may include lists of groups and organizations that can provide support, specialized expertise, and even equipment. Building true collaborative relationships with partners will require ongoing or at least regular interaction with credible partners.

It Is Possible to Coordinate and Cooperate With Hostile Groups?

Many crises can result in angry feelings, even hostility, among the groups an organization needs to coordinate with. These may be groups that have been harmed by the crisis. Is it possible to work with those groups? In most cases, it is possible to discover some basis for working together by finding common values and common ground and by acknowledging the anger people are feeling. Sometimes organizations have to face people who are angry and who have been harmed by a crisis. This may happen in community meetings, press conferences, and even annual meetings. These interactions are generally intense and unpleasant and sometimes become very hostile. In cases like this, it is unlikely a collaborative relationship can develop, but organizations and hostile groups can coordinate their efforts, perhaps to help those who have been harmed or to distribute important information. In addition, even the act of listening—trying to understand the views of others and looking for ways to cooperate—can be helpful in reducing outrage and creating more effective relationships. Even when groups are angry and hostile, we believe it is important to make the effort to coordinate and collaborate.

Summary

Collaborating and coordinating with credible sources and partners are almost always necessary for an effective crisis response. Developing these relationships before a crisis begins will improve its reputation and create a reservoir of goodwill it can draw on during a crisis. Collaborating and coordinating will also help to create consistent messages and can be important in getting important resources to manage a crisis. Although this may be one of the more difficult best practices, it is one of the most important. Collaborating and coordinating mean an organization will not have to face the crisis alone. Through collaboration and coordination, stakeholders, partners, experts, and credible sources of information will be there to assist in managing the crisis.

Key Takeaways for Collaborating and Coordinating

1) Collaboration means working with others to achieve some outcome. Coordination involves unifying activities to create a common outcome. Collaboration usually requires working more closely than coordination does.

2) One of the most persistent challenges during a crisis is coordinating and collaborating with other groups, agencies, communities, and stakeholders. Failure to coordinate and collaborate can make a crisis much worse, but successfully working with others can provide much needed resources to a response.

3) Establishing networks of partnerships can occur before a crisis happens as part of a larger crisis plan. This allows organizations to develop relationships that can be very helpful in managing a crisis.

4) Establishing relationships with credible partners can help improve the organization's own reputation. Groups, agencies, and organizations with specialized expertise, connections with specific communities, and who do not have conflicts of interest are generally good partners during a crisis.

5) Coordination and collaboration can be built on different areas of skill and expertise, different role assignments, or different regions. Regardless of how coordination and collaboration are achieved, they are almost always necessary for an effective crisis response because few organizations or communities have the resources to manage a crisis on their own.

References

Federal Emergency Management Agency. (2016). Glossary. Retrieved from https://emilms.fema.gov/is200b/glossary.htm

Frandsen, F., & Johansen, W. (2015). Organizations, stakeholders, and intermediaries: Towards a general theory. *International Journal of Strategic Communication, 9*(4), 253–271.

Grunig, J. E. (2001). Two-way symmetrical public relations: Past, present, and future. In R. L. Heath (Ed.), *Handbook of public relations* (pp. 11–30). Thousand Oaks, CA: Sage.

Jones, G. H., Jones, B. H., & Little, P. (2000). Reputation as reservoir: Buffering against loss in times of economic crisis. *Corporate Reputation Review, 3*(1), 21–29.

Quarantelli, E. L. (1982). What is a disaster? In B. Jones, & M. Tomazevic (Eds.), *Social and economic aspects of earthquake* (pp. 453–465). Ithaca, NY: Cornell University Press.

Spence, P. R., & Lachlan, K. A. (2016). Reoccurring challenges and emerging threats: Crises and the new millennium. In A. Schwarz, M. W. Seeger, & C. Auer (Eds.), *The handbook of international crisis communication research* (pp. 212–223). West Sussex, UK: Wiley.

8

Media Access

Meet the Needs of the Media and Remain Accessible

Best practices of crisis communicators are based on principles of effective communication with a variety of groups, communities, and stakeholders, including the media. The media—radio, television, and print—is a primary way to reach the public. During a crisis, the media is obligated to report accurately and completely. Social media can provide very direct communication during a crisis and we recommend social media be part of any crisis communication plan. Traditional, or what is sometimes called legacy, media includes journalism. According to the American Press Institute (2017), journalism is "the activity of gathering, assessing, creating, and presenting news and information" (n.p.).

During a crisis, reporters strive to tell the story of what is happening, report the facts accurately, and be sensitive to the people who are harmed by the crisis. There are many cases where news reporting was very important in helping crisis decision makers and individuals affected by the crisis understand what was happening. There are many cases where reporters have risked their lives to report on crises. During a crisis, journalists are sometimes aggressive in trying to get the facts, and crisis managers sometimes see them as adversaries. The term "fake news" has been used as a way to call into question the accuracy and credibility of journalism. Reporters working for established media are usually trained professionals who work very hard to confirm their stories. They follow high professional and ethical standards and they perform a critical service to society. Although the confusion and uncertainty surrounding a crisis make it hard to get the story, and get the facts straight, journalists are generally committed to objective reporting.

Rather than viewing the media and journalists as the enemy in a crisis situation, crisis communicators should engage the media. This is the

Communication in Times of Trouble: Best Practices for Crisis and Emergency Risk Communication, First Edition. Matthew W. Seeger and Timothy L. Sellnow.
© 2019 John Wiley & Sons, Inc. Published 2019 by John Wiley & Sons, Inc.

only way the organization can get its side of the story out. This includes being open and honest and communicating quickly so the media can be a strategic resource for managing the crisis. Meeting the needs of the media and remaining open and accessible is a best practice of crisis communication.

Why Is Media Access Important?

A crisis creates an immediate and usually intense need for information about what is happening and what people should do in response. Providing information quickly can reduce the level of harm, and it is the responsibility of the organization associated with the crisis to communicate as much information as they can. A crisis is usually seen as breaking news, a story that is currently occurring or developing and a story that requires immediate coverage (Lewis, 2008). If an organization can respond quickly and tell the public what is happening, it can get out in front of the story and establish that it is the best source of information about the crisis. This can be a very important advantage in a crisis circumstance. If information is not available, concern will grow, rumors may start to circulate, and, in some cases, more people may be harmed. Delaying the release of information is also likely to hurt the image of the organization.

Radio, television, print media, and digital media are the primary ways information is disseminated to the public. Radio is a very accessible and immediate way to reach the general public. Many people can access radios in their cars, allowing them to get updates even when they are evacuating. Radio is also a resilient communication technology and can be used in very flexible ways. In some cases, local radio stations have essentially become crisis information centers, with people calling in with their questions that are then answered by emergency management professionals. Television and video coverage can also be immediate. Distributing images and videos of a crisis can help people understand the scope and impact of a crisis. Information is also necessary to help people understand what they should do. After Hurricane Katrina flooded New Orleans, television coverage of the crisis was very important in helping people understand the extent of the damage. Pictures and videos can also help generate support and assistance for those affected by a crisis. Media reports during a crisis help people understand how they can protect themselves. Weather reporters covering extreme weather events often include information about sheltering in place or evacuating. Sometimes, weather reporters will include other information about how people can reduce their risks, including boiling water, avoiding certain areas, identifying the best evacuation routes, and preparing personal emergency kits.

Digital media, including Twitter, Facebook, YouTube, and various websites, are used by journalists both as sources of information and as ways to tell the story of a crisis. These forms of communication allow the people who are experiencing crisis to report directly on what they are experiencing. Sometimes, these people are called citizen journalists. Blogs, Twitter, and Facebook allow citizens to actively participate in the process of journalism. This includes collecting, reporting, analyzing, and disseminating news and information, often in real time. Sometimes these citizen journalists are called first communicators in reference to the role played by first responders to a crisis. Citizens can provide reports that include timely, independent, reliable, accurate, and relevant information (Bowman & Willis, 2003). In one case, a small local citizen-based website called Rim of the World provided the most up-to-date information about the 2007 wildfires spreading through San Diego (Novak & Vidoloff, 2011). This citizen-run website became the most important site for disaster information. Through the widespread use of smartphones, people can easily share photos, videos, and eyewitness reports as a crisis unfolds. Because it is sometimes hard for journalists to get into a crisis zone, citizen journalism often provides the most accurate, up-to-date information, especially early in the crisis. Citizen journalism during a crisis has the additional advantage of allowing people affected by a crisis to speak for themselves, which sometimes includes asking for help.

Although citizen journalism and the participation of people experiencing the crisis are very valuable, professional journalism and established news sources are still important. News organizations have more resources and can check facts, provide background, conduct in-depth investigations, and reach broader audiences quickly. Journalists are trained observers and know how to assemble facts in ways people can understand. They are often seen as more credible than other sources, such as Facebook or Twitter. However, most news outlets—radio, television, and print—also have a very active online presence and will post news reports to their websites and Twitter feeds. The government agencies responding to crises, such as the police and fire departments, will also have active Twitter accounts they will use during a crisis. In reality, established media journalism and citizen journalism often work together during a crisis. Managers should remain accessible to both. Even when people first learn about a crisis through social media, they often turn to more established media outlets to confirm the story (Anthony, Sellnow, & Millner, 2013).

What Does Accessibility Mean?

During the chaos and confusion of a crisis, it is not always easy to give media the access they want. Sometimes, the crisis zone cannot be easily or safely accessed. Crisis managers are busy responding to an event and understandably do not want to take time out to talk to journalists. Sometimes managers are concerned that talking to the press may increase their legal liability and create more problems later on. In other cases, managers have not been trained to face the press and are uncomfortable doing so under stressful conditions where they may not have all the facts. Sometimes, journalists are seen as threatening.

Accessibility does not necessarily require having all the facts or answers about the crisis. Especially during the early stages of a crisis, journalists will not expect organizations to know everything about what happened, to know why the crisis happened, or to know what will be done in response. What journalists do expect is that organizations will try to get the answers and that they will share information when they have it. Accessibility is a commitment to cooperate with the media to get the information and share it with the public through regular updates. This usually requires that organizations work with the media during a crisis. This is easier when journalists and managers understand each other's roles and responsibilities and trust one another. Journalists have an obligation to get the story, to verify facts, and to disseminate them as quickly as possible to publics. This includes information that can help people protect themselves during a crisis, such as evacuation notices, boil water notices, food recalls, or where to go to get help. Although reporters sometimes get the story wrong and sometimes act in ways that are not professional, these are the exceptions to the way the media generally covers a crisis.

As we noted previously, partnerships with the public is a best practice of crisis communication. Working together with the media can be one important partnership. We also think of accessibility as a process that can begin before a crisis happens and extends after the crisis is over. Many organizations try to build relationships with journalists before a crisis. Some organizations host media days where reporters are invited to visit the organization, meet new organizational leaders, and observe new operations. As we noted, organizations may invite reporters to observe and even participate in crisis drills and exercises. Such proactive relationship building is helpful to both organizations and reporters. Organizations have an opportunity to establish trusting relationships with reporters in advance of any problems, and reporters identify the key sources they will need to contact when reporting on possible crises in the future. This can help reporters cover crises more accurately and effectively if and when they occur.

How Does an Organization Maintain Accessibility?

Accessibility and openness with the media are not just one thing. Rather, they are a process that develops as a crisis unfolds over time. Openness is a way to maintain two-way communication and a symmetrical relationship with the media and, through the media, with key stakeholders (Grunig & Hunt, 1984). This approach can help build mutual understanding and trust. Accessibility involves a variety of activities, structures, and outcomes.

When communicating with the media, organizations should avoid the appearance of inconsistency by accepting the uncertainty that comes with a crisis and resisting the temptation to offer overly reassuring messages. During the initial stages of a crisis, before all the facts are known, it is often tempting to downplay any possible harm and play up the impression that everything is under control. As we described earlier, these kinds of overly reassuring statements often are later demonstrated not to be correct. When that happens, organizations are forced to backtrack, which can hurt their credibility. It is often easier to offer initial statements such as, "Based on what we currently know" or "The facts are still coming in and we don't yet know the extent of the damage." It is important to follow these statements with commitments to get all the facts out as soon as they are available. We discuss these strategies further in a later section.

Media training of top executives, completed by crisis communicators prior to the onset of a crisis, can also help create openness and accessibility. Many public relations agencies and government groups provide training for their leaders. Crisis spokespersons should be identified and trained as part of precrisis planning. When spokespersons and top managers have been trained, they are more confident and they know what to expect. They understand that reporters have a job to do and they are less likely to become argumentative or defensive. When spokespersons become defensive, they can create the impression they have something to hide.

Care should also be taken to reach out to multiple media outlets. As we noted earlier, most media outlets will maintain a very active social media presence and they will usually post and tweet about breaking news. Using multiple media sources also increases the chances the information will reach underrepresented populations. It is sometimes tempting during a crisis to focus attention on television and ignore print reporters, but many smaller newspapers and print media outlets reach ethnic or minority communities, and many of these groups will have important websites and groups of Twitter followers. It is also important to remember that local media will still be around even after national media have left. These smaller, more localized media can be very important audiences during a crisis. In addition, print media typically will follow a story longer and will report in more depth. This may include follow-up after the immediate crisis stage has passed.

There are specific procedures organizations can follow to help create openness and accessibility. Most organizations will hold press conferences and issue press statements, including providing background information, sets of frequently asked questions, and guidance statements. This free flow of information is important to maintaining openness and accessibility. Press conferences during crises and question and answer sessions that typically occur can be very helpful in creating an open and accessible communication environment and the free flow of information. The opportunities to follow up and offer clarification can reduce misunderstandings and inaccuracies. It is important to remember, however, that during a press conference, reporters can ask anything they want, so spokespersons need to be prepared for uncomfortable questions. Some reporters do go out of their way to ask very hard questions and some even pride themselves on being confrontational. It is important not to get caught up in arguments with reporters, even when they are being unfair. The best approach is to answer questions as truthfully and as honestly as possible and offer to follow up with additional information.

Holding a press conference requires careful planning. We described preevent planning as our second best practice, and crisis plans should include information about press conferences. When planning a press conference, it is important to have an appropriate place that is safe and accessible and to ensure that details such as parking, electrical outlets, Internet access, coffee, and even restroom facilities are considered. Location can be a problem during a crisis because the crisis zone may not be secure. Television reporters will need visuals and will need to set up cameras. Most organizations issue media advisories to announce press conferences. During a large-scale crisis, standing press conferences may be scheduled, for example, every afternoon. These schedules should also take into account the deadlines most reporters have for filing their stories. It may also be appropriate to consider remote access to press conferences through video or audio links. Recording a press conference can be very helpful in making sure all agreements to provide additional information occur. In many cases, the designated spokesperson for the press conference will be supported by others, such as other members of the organization or another emergency management professional working on the crisis.

Another structure that can help ensure openness and accessibility is the Joint Information Center or Joint Information System (JIS). According to the Federal Emergency Management Agency (FEMA), the JIS is a "mechanism to organize, integrate, and coordinate information to ensure timely, accurate, accessible, and consistent messaging across multiple jurisdictions and/or disciplines with nongovernmental organizations and the private sector" (FEMA, 2007, n.p.). A JIS is a committee or location that brings all the crisis communicators together so they can coordinate communication activities. Coordination includes agreeing on the content of messages and the timing of their release.

What Happens If Organizations Are Not Open During a Crisis?

Being open and accessible during a crisis is not easy. Crises are vulnerable and risky times for organizations and for managers. Individual managers may fear they will be blamed for the crisis. In these circumstances, there is sometimes a natural tendency to "batten down the hatches" and limit access. Sometimes managers decide the best approach is to close themselves off from any outside information so they aren't distracted. Although this may seem like a good way to protect the organization, this approach is a very defensive position. In most cases, being closed off from outside sources of information is an ineffective and even dangerous approach to a crisis. Maintaining an open free flow of information during a crisis allows an organization to understand how the crisis is developing, how people are responding, and what information is needed. Accessibility and openness are a two-way communication process that allows the organization to adjust its strategy as new information becomes available. The media can be one of the most important sources of information.

When organizations fail to be open and accessible during a crisis, they also limit their ability to tell their own story and speak for themselves. This does not mean the story will go unreported. Reporters will still find other sources of information, but the organization's perspective will not be represented. During a crisis, there is an intense need for information, what we have called an "information vacuum." If the organization does not help fill that vacuum, another source of information will. Reporters will seek out employees, members of the community, emergency response officials, subject matter experts, and others for information. When this happens, the organization is usually forced to respond or react to the story. A reactive position is much less effective than getting out ahead of the story of the crisis from a proactive position. In addition, once alternative sources of information have been identified, they will be used again and again.

As we mentioned previously, when organizations are not open and accessible early in the crisis, it can create the impression they have something to hide. In these cases, reporters may feel they need to dig deeper to find out what is really happening. This added scrutiny from the press can lead to additional negative news coverage and extend the news story of the crisis. In general, the longer the media coverage goes on, the greater the potential for causing additional harm to the organization's image and reputation. It is typically most effective to get as much information, accurate information, out as quickly as possible so the duration of the media coverage is as short as possible. Being open and accessible with the media can help an organization get past the story quickly.

Will the Media Tell a Negative Story Regardless of the Facts?

As with any profession, there are some reporters with questionable ethics. Some media outlets look for the most sensational story and adopt the attitude that dramatic and sensational stories will always be the most newsworthy. The philosophy of "If it bleeds it leads" as a news story takes advantage of fear and tries to grab the publics' attention (Serani, 2011). Most news outlets are for-profit organizations and larger audiences mean increased revenue. For the most part, however, reporters and organizational managers can and should cooperate during a crisis. Readers and viewers typically turn to both traditional and new media sources to learn as much as they can during a crisis. Thus, cooperating with reporters creates an opportunity for organizations to efficiently share vital information with their publics.

Summary

The media is a vital resource for distributing information to the diverse publics affected by a crisis. Rather than viewing the media as the enemy in a crisis situation, spokespersons should engage multiple media outlets and promptly share relevant information as it becomes available. This approach helps the organization take a proactive stance in response to a crisis. Research reveals that most media reporters prioritize the well-being of their readers and viewers in reporting on crises. Establishing relationships and even partnerships with the media as part of crisis planning is advised.

Key Takeaways for Media Access

1) Rather than viewing the media and journalists as the enemy in a crisis situation, crisis communicators should engage the media. During a crisis, reporters play an important role in sharing information about the crisis and in helping individuals affected by the crisis understand what is happening.

2) Organizations should interact with both traditional media sources such as television, radio, and newspapers as well as new media sources whose online coverage is widely read by people affected by or concerned about the crisis.

3) Granting accessibility does not necessarily require having all the facts or answers about the crisis. In the early stages of a crisis, journalists cannot expect organizations to know everything about what happened, to know why the crisis happened, or to know what will be done in response. Journalists do, however, expect that organizations will share information at regular intervals when they have it.

4) Being open and accessible with the media requires organizations to engage in two-way communication with reporters by answering questions and being open to feedback. Care should also be taken to reach out to multiple media outlets without exclusion or favoritism.

5) An unfortunate reaction of some organizations may be to conceal the crisis in hopes of avoiding public criticism. Maintaining an open free flow of information during a crisis, however, allows an organization to better understand how the crisis is developing, how people are responding, and what information is needed.

References

American Press Institute. (2017). What is journalism? Retrieved from https://www.americanpressinstitute.org/journalism-essentials/what-is-journalism

Anthony, K. E., Sellnow, T. L., & Millner, A. G. (2013). Message convergence as a message-centered approach to analyzing and improving risk communication. *Journal of Applied Communication Research, 41,* 346–364.

Bowman, S., & Willis, C. (2003). We media: How audiences are shaping the future of news and information. Retrieved from http://www.hypergene.net/wemedia/download/we_media.pdf

Federal Emergency Management Agency. (2007). Basic guidance for public information officers (PIOs). Retrieved from https://www.fema.gov/media-library-data/20130726-1623-20490-0276/basic_guidance_for_pios_final_draft_12_06_07.pdf

Grunig, J. E., & Hunt, T. T. (1984). *Managing public relations.* New York, NY: Holt, Rinehart and Winston.

Lewis, M. (2008). Breaking news. In M. W. Seeger, T. L. Sellnow, & R. R. Ulmer (Eds.), *Crisis communication and the public health.* New York, NY: Hampton Press.

Novak, J. M., & Vidoloff, K. G. (2011). New frames on crisis: Citizen journalism changing the dynamics of crisis communication. *International Journal of Mass Emergencies & Disasters, 29*(3), 181–202.

Serani, D. (2011, June 7). If it bleeds, it leads: Understanding fear-based media. *Psychology Today.* Retrieved from https://www.psychologytoday.com/us/blog/two-takes-depression/201106/if-it-bleeds-it-leads-understanding-fear-based-media

9

Compassion

Communicate With Compassion

Whether communicating with publics, media, or their employees, designated spokespersons should demonstrate appropriate levels of compassion. Such compassion includes expressing concern for those affected or at risk and an empathetic willingness to see the crisis through their eyes (Covello, 2003). This need for emotional sensitivity constitutes our eighth best practice. The expression of compassion by a crisis spokesperson is a vital characteristic that enhances messenger and message credibility (Simpson, Clegg, & Pinae Cunha, 2013). Publics respond much more positively to spokespersons who acknowledge their concerns and demonstrate understanding and compassion for any harm that may have occurred. If publics see an expression of genuine concern and empathy, they have more faith that the actions taken or recommended by the spokesperson are appropriate and in their best interest.

Despite the nearly universal support for expressing compassion in crisis situations (Simpson et al., 2013), some crisis spokespersons may be reluctant to include such expressions for fear of appearing weak or unprofessional. Moreover, some refuse to express such emotions out of concern that their words will be used against them in future litigation. These efforts to maintain pride and professionalism or legal distance are often perceived by publics as cold and uncaring (Liska, Petrun, Sellnow, & Seeger, 2012). The resulting perception of such self-indulgence, however, may undermine the message and credibility of the messenger.

A compassionate expression of concern and empathy reframes the crisis-related message to prioritize the needs of publics. Anthony and Sellnow (2011) characterized this audience-centered focus as a reflection

Communication in Times of Trouble: Best Practices for Crisis and Emergency Risk Communication, First Edition. Matthew W. Seeger and Timothy L. Sellnow.
© 2019 John Wiley & Sons, Inc. Published 2019 by John Wiley & Sons, Inc.

of C. S. Lewis' (1985) declaration that, "You can't get second things by putting them first; you can get second things only by putting the first things first" (p. 22). In crisis situations, the physical and emotional well-being of those affected by the crisis is the priority or a "first thing." Concerns about profit, legality, or other self-interests are secondary. These secondary concerns are not compromised by sharing concern for the well-being of those whose lives are disrupted by crisis (Anthony & Sellnow, 2011). Rather, an expression of genuine compassion early in a crisis can enhance the spokesperson's credibility throughout the crisis recovery.

Coombs (1999) cautions that "compassion should not be taken as a cure-all response" because, although it has benefits, compassion "also can be a drain on stock prices" (p. 139). In response to this concern, we emphasize the point that a compassionate response should be provided out of genuine concern for all those affected by the crisis. Certainly, actions that address reputational matters and threaten stock prices are expected in the latter stages of a crisis. In the early stages of a crisis, however, messages of compassion should precede efforts to improve one's reputation and protect the bottom line. Failure to do so is placing the second thing (stock prices) ahead of the first thing (well-being of those affected by the crisis). As C. S. Lewis (1985) explains, two things may both be good, but pursuing something secondary over something primary inevitably results in the loss of both.

What Is a Compassionate Response to Crisis?

Though crisis communication situations vary widely, the central elements of compassion remain consistent. Lu & Schuldt (2016) identify three essential and consistent characteristics of compassionate crisis communication. They explain "compassion is a prosocial emotion that is linked to increased care and concern for others, decreased attention to one's own needs, and a motivation to aid another person for their own sake" (p. 193). This three-part definition provides a practical framework for spokespersons.

First, compassionate crisis communication is based in an "increased care and concern for others" (Lu & Schuldt, 2016, p. 193). By their nature, crises create hardship. This hardship is often experienced by innocent bystanders of the crisis. For example, a Canadian Pacific Railway freight train derailment near Minot, N.D., resulted in a ruptured anhydrous ammonia tanker car, releasing a poisonous cloud of the chemical that settled over the city. The poisonous gas injured at least 60 residents and killed 1 (Witte, 2002). The governor of North Dakota at the time, John Hoeven, quickly acknowledged the shock and fear the residents were feeling and pledged assistance to the community. Canadian Pacific Railway was much slower in reaching out to the community. Hoeven's compassionate response brought an initial sense of order to the residents who were experiencing a crisis far beyond their control. He anticipated their needs and sought to reassure the community by promising to provide the resources for the urgent health care they needed and to protect them from further physical harm due to the derailment. The governor's message preceded any discussion of blame or responsibility. His foremost concern was helping those in need.

Second, compassionate crisis communication expresses "decreased attention to one's own needs" (Lu & Schuldt, 2016, p. 193). Compassionate messages precede any actions that could create a perception the organization is being forced by legal or regulatory policies to take corrective actions following a crisis. Instead, compassionate crisis communication expresses a degree of selflessness on the part of the spokesperson and organization. British Petroleum (BP) chief executive officer (CEO) Tony Hayward completely missed this point when, in an interview during the acute phase of the colossal oil spill in the Gulf of Mexico, he asserted, "I want my life back" as his primary justification for resolving the crisis (Reuters, 2010). Hayward was condemned for what residents perceived as an insensitive and self-centered remark that represented his lack of commitment to the communities whose livelihoods were disrupted or destroyed by the crisis. By contrast, Tom Kilgore, CEO and president of the Tennessee Valley Authority (TVA), was far more compassionate in his initial response to a coal ash spill that devastated communities along a stretch of the Emory River near Knoxville, Tenn. The damage was horrific and Kilgore placed his full attention on the communities affected by the crisis. He acknowledged that TVA could never return the region to its pristine existence or make the community "whole" again ("Tennessee: Community Awaits Answers," 2009, para. 6). He pledged to address residents' immediate needs, to engage the TVA in a wide-scale and unprecedented cleanup process, and to fully investigate internal procedures at TVA to identify the failures that led to the crisis. Sadly, BP's and TVA's cleanup activities will continue for many years in both the Gulf of Mexico and Tennessee. Unlike Hayward, however, Kilgore remained a central figure in the cleanup process for several years.

Third, compassionate crisis communication exhibits a "motivation to aid another person for their own sake" (Lu & Schuldt, 2016, p. 193). Schwan's response to a *Salmonella* outbreak in its ice cream provides a classic example of offering to aid others solely for their sake. After seeing a pattern of salmonellosis in its customers, Schwan's voluntarily recalled all ice cream products. Before any investigation was completed, Schwan's also pledged to pay the medical bills of customers who sought treatment for salmonellosis. Schwan's also asked its door-to-door delivery drivers to personally solicit returns of tainted merchandise and to provide refunds. This response further intensified the strong loyalty many consumers had for the company (Sellnow, Ulmer, & Snider, 1998). A later investigation found that one of Schwan's external suppliers was to blame for the outbreak.

Who Is the Best Organizational Spokesperson for Expressing Compassion?

Selecting a crisis spokesperson should not be based solely on the organizational hierarchy or information specialization. Rather, organizations "should choose a person capable of delivering your messages with the compassion and care that a crisis demands" (Phillips, 2013, para. 7). The spokesperson must also have access to essential information and the capacity to withstand the rigors of intense scrutiny from reporters. Maintaining a compassionate focus in the face of media questions can be challenging. Communication consultant Kim Harrison advises spokespersons to remain "compassionate, empathetic, courteous, and considerate" throughout the process (n.d., para. 15). The challenge is that "it's not easy to do this under pressure when silly questions are asked or repeated, but this patient approach is necessary" (Harrison, n.d., para. 15). A spokesperson could indeed genuinely care very deeply for the well-being of the organization's stakeholders, but lapses of impatience or intolerance in reaction to the relentless probes of reporters can lead to nonverbal expressions of insincerity.

As the crisis moves on from the initial stage, multiple internal spokespersons are likely to be featured to discuss the details of the recovery or cleanup. These spokespersons will emerge based on the informational needs at any given point in the crisis recovery. The emphasis on compassion should not dissolve as new spokespersons and evidence related to the crisis appear. Rather, compassion should remain a consistent feature expressed by all spokespersons during all stages of the crisis. To accomplish this task, providing media training for all spokespersons is advised. Such media training should emphasize simulated crisis circumstances where the organization's message is challenged. Specifically, this training should include mock interviews that challenge the organization's spokesperson to maintain a compassionate disposition when asked questions that are accusatory, technically complex, misinformed, or mundane. Training of this nature can prepare spokespersons for the inevitable challenges of media interviews.

When Is Expressing Compassion Most Important?

We accept that showing compassion can improve or maintain an organization's reputation; however, reputation should not be the primary motivation. As we discussed, once a crisis has occurred, expressing sincere compassion for those affected by the crisis should precede any tactical effort to rebuild the organization's image. Thus, the obvious answer to the question of when to show compassion in a crisis is immediately. Displaying compassion should not, however, be reserved for the onset of crises. Simpson et al. (2013) caution against showing compassion for the first time when a crisis occurs. Instead, they argue that compassion should be a consistent element of an organization's external communication. They see compassion as "ongoing social relational processes best cultivated in times of normality, rather than in moments of disaster" (p. 123). In their research, they found organizations that were most responsive in crisis situations "already had compassionate policies and routines in place as an ongoing mode of practice" (p. 120). These ongoing compassionate policies were regularly monitored and altered through ongoing feedback provided by the organizations' stakeholders.

Enacting compassionate policies that are featured continuously in the life of an organization has multiple benefits. Considerable evidence indicates that organizations seen as having corporate social responsibility are often preferred by consumers (Dodd & Supa, 2011). From a crisis communication perspective, corporate social responsibility is reflected in an organization's ongoing compassionate policies and actions that show concern for their publics and the environment. These compassionate acts can, as we discussed earlier, build a "reservoir of goodwill" in the eyes of publics (Ulmer, Sellnow, & Seeger, 2017). Organizations that have accumulated a reservoir of goodwill can draw upon these positive impressions when they face crises. The result is a greater tendency by publics to give the organization the benefit of the doubt and to trust that the organization is sincere in pledging to prioritize the well-being of their stakeholders when responding to crises. The short answer as to when to show compassion in a crisis is immediately; however, the longer, more accurate answer is to show compassion through an ongoing effort to function as a socially responsible organization.

Should an Organization Express Compassion If Blame Is Uncertain?

In the early stages of crises, the inherent lack of information makes assigning blame difficult. What is not difficult to promptly recognize, however, is the stakeholders who are at risk or are suffering. Organizations that reach out to their stakeholders early in crises, whether the organization is or is not to blame, contribute to their reservoir of goodwill. In fact, Englehardt, Sallot, and Springston (2004) explain that organizations stand to benefit from what they call "compassion with blame" (p. 127). This strategy involves expressing concern for publics who are suffering because of the crisis and, if possible, offering assistance without accepting blame. Enacting a strategy of compassion without blame does not prohibit an organization from accepting blame once a crisis investigation is completed. Rather, this approach allows organizations to behave in a compassionate, socially conscious way without fear of incriminating themselves. As we discussed, Schwan's began compensating customers' medical expenses before a full understanding of how the crisis originated was available. The legal aspects of the case lingered on for years, but Schwan's words and actions early in the crisis created an enduring sense of social responsibility in the minds of their customers (Sellnow et al., 1998).

How Should an Organization Express Compassion If Blame Is Certain?

In cases where blame is clearly established for an organization, compassion can be shown through the actions the organization takes to resolve the crisis (Benoit, 2015). Specifically, organizations accepting blame for a crisis can show compassion in three steps:

1) Showing empathy for those affected by the crisis.
2) Outlining specific corrective actions.
3) Engaging in mortification (asking for forgiveness).

An apology for blame should begin with a recognition of the pain the crisis caused and an expression of genuine remorse for this pain. Having established this recognition and remorse, an organization can introduce corrective actions that, first, fulfill the needs of those who are affected by the crisis, and, second, explain how the organization will "mend its ways" in the future to avoid a repeat of such incidents (Benoit, 2015, p. 26). This strategy moves well beyond simple compensation to those victimized by crisis. Compensation can be done begrudgingly or to sidestep blame, neither of which show compassion. Mortification is a clear admission of guilt with an appeal for forgiveness. If organizations succeed in completing these three steps, the hope is "audiences will forgive, but forgiveness is not certain" (Benoit, 2015, p. 27). Still, an organization whose blame is certain is unlikely to improve its reputation or legal standing by refusing to show compassion for its stakeholders (Choi & Lin, 2009).

How Should Spokespersons Express Compassion Through Social Media?

Social media is both friend and enemy to organizations responding to crises. Frandsen and Johansen (2017) explain that social media can help organizations "quickly share crisis responses, instruction, and updates with stakeholders on both its corporate website and on stakeholders' networks" (p. 171). On the other hand, any missteps by the organization can be shared thousands of times through social networks before the organization can offer a response. Despite the potential pitfalls of social media, organizations cannot ignore this opportunity for sharing compassionate messages during crises. North, Li, Liu, and Ji (2018) contend that in crisis situations, "speed and sincerity are still vital and perhaps more so now with the rapidity and permanence—thanks to screenshots—of social media" (p. 207). Accordingly, organizations should plan to have a social media presence for all relevant stakeholders when responding to crises.

Lachlan, Spence, and Lin (2018) encourage organizations to "reconsider their assumptions about how to best reach audiences in times of crisis and emergency" (p. 296). This reconsideration goes beyond simply delivering the same statement or press release shared with traditional media over a social media channel. Instead, organizations can show compassion for their stakeholders during crises by capitalizing on the opportunities for two-way communication or dialog via social media. We discussed the importance of dialog in connecting messages with publics in an earlier chapter. Organizations can engage in dialog by using social media platforms, like Twitter, to listen and attend to stakeholder responses to the organization's initial messages. Unfortunately, many organizations fail to capitalize on this opportunity for public dialog. Instead, many organizations use social media "in the same manner as they would broadcast instead of holding dialogs with stakeholders" (Lachlan et al., 2018, p. 310). To express compassion through dialog, organizations must dedicate sufficient resources to two areas. First, they should share fitting messages over social media platforms. Second, they should collect, sort, and respond to the responses received either as themes or in individual replies. By doing so, organizations exploit the speed and broad distribution of social media while maintaining a sincere commitment to addressing the needs of those whose lives are disrupted by the crisis.

What Role Does Culture Play in the Expression of Compassion?

Spokespersons can show compassion by adapting their message to meet the distinct needs of their multiple publics. Audience analysis focusing on differences ranging from family composition, religion, and language preference to age, income, and education level all have the potential to create disparate needs from factions within a greater audience. Those spokespersons who tailor or adapt their messages to meet the needs of their diverse audiences foster greater trust and are more influential (Sellnow, Sellnow, Lane, & Littlefield, 2012). For example, hurricane warnings that urge people in threatened areas to evacuate are not received universally within the target population. Those who have the financial capacity to purchase gasoline, rent a room, purchase restaurant food along the way, and cover other expenses are more likely to evacuate. Those who are financially challenged may lack the tangible means to evacuate. Evacuation shelters may be available at no expense; however, finding transportation to the shelter, perceived safety within the shelter, and the willingness of the shelter to harbor pets all play a role in whether or not individuals will evacuate their threatened homes. Spokespersons show compassion when they acknowledge these challenges and communicate strategies for overcoming them.

Spokespersons also show compassion by addressing cultural differences within their audiences. Different culture manifests in how people communicate. This creates a need for spokespersons to adapt their crisis communication to acknowledge these differences (Kwansah-Aidoo & George, 2017). For culturally diverse audiences, spokespersons show compassion by tailoring their messages to make their content culturally centered. Many spokespersons take culture into consideration when sharing crisis messages. To be culture centered, however, spokespersons must move beyond being culture neutral or expressing cultural sensitivity (Dutta, 2007). Spokespersons are culture neutral when they assume all cultural groups within the intended audience will respond to the message in the same way. A culturally sensitive approach is achieved when spokespersons recognize the characteristics of the population and create messages that meet the needs of each group. The most compassionate level is the culture-centered approach. In culture-centered communication, members from underrepresented populations are directly consulted about the content and channels for distributing crisis messages. To reach the culture-centered level, organizations must cultivate relationships with underrepresented populations and include them in their crisis planning (Littlefield, 2013).

Summary

During a crisis, the designated leader or spokesperson will often be asked to speak to publics and media. The spokesperson may assume that sticking to the facts and avoiding any emotion is safer from a legal or professional perspective. In this case, publics may get the impression the spokesperson is cold and uncaring. Although false emotion can backfire, spokespersons should be willing to express human feelings during a crisis. It is almost always appropriate to say, "We express our deep concern for anyone harmed, and we are sorry for any harm that may have occurred." This kind of statement is natural whenever a serious crisis has occurred, be it a defective product or a case of workplace violence. Spokespersons should demonstrate appropriate levels of compassion, concern, and empathy when communicating with their publics, media, and employees. Expressions of genuine concern and empathy tend to give publics and employees faith that the actions underway or recommended are in their best interest. A failure to show compassion can create an impression of distance or insensitivity. Regardless of who is selected as the organization's crisis spokesperson, expressing compassion is essential.

Key Takeaways for Communicating With Compassion

1) Whether communicating with publics, media, or their employees, designated spokespersons should communicate compassionately to express concern for those affected or at risk and an empathetic willingness to see the crisis through their eyes.

2) In crisis situations, the physical and emotional well-being of those affected by the crisis is the priority or a "first thing." Concerns about profit, legality, or other self-interests are secondary. These secondary concerns are not compromised by sharing concern for the well-being of those whose lives are disrupted by crisis. On the contrary, prioritizing secondary concerns while people are suffering can do lasting damage to an organization's reputation.

---

3) Organizations should meet three criteria when communicating compassionately: increased care and concern for others, decreased attention to one's own needs, and a motivation to aid another person for their own sake.

4) Selecting a crisis spokesperson should not be based solely on the organizational hierarchy or information specialization. Rather, organizations should select a spokesperson who is capable of remaining compassionate, empathetic, courteous, and considerate despite the criticism, warranted or unwarranted, that often arises during crisis situations.

5) Organizations can and should express compassion early in crisis situations whether blame for the crisis is certain or uncertain.

References

Anthony, K. E., & Sellnow, T. L. (2011). Beyond Narnia: The necessity of C.S. Lewis' *First and Second Things* in applied communication research. *Journal of Applied Communication Research, 39,* 441–443.

Benoit, W. L. (2015). *Accounts, excuses, and apologies* (2nd ed.). Albany, NY: SUNY Press.

Choi, Y., & Lin, Y. H. (2009). Individual difference in crisis response perception: How do legal experts and lay people perceive apology and compassion responses? *Public Relations Review, 35,* 452–454.

Coombs, T. W. (1999). Information and compassion in crisis responses: A test of their effects. *Journal of Public Relations Research, 112,* 125–142.

Covello, V. T. (2003). Best practices in public health risk and crisis communication. *Journal of Health Communication, 8*(S1), 5–8.

Dodd, M. D., & Supa, D. W. (2011). Understanding the effect of corporate social responsibility on consumer purchase intention. *Public Relations Journal, 5*(3), 1–19.

Dutta, M. J. (2007). Communicating about culture and health: Theorizing culture-centered and cultural sensitivity approaches. *Communication Theory, 17,* 304–328.

Englehardt, K. J., Sallot, L. M., & Springston, J. K. (2004). Compassion without blame: Testing the accident decision flow chart with the crash of ValuJet flight 592. *Journal of Public Relations Research, 16*(2), 127–156.

Frandsen, F., & Johansen, W. (2017). *Organizational crisis communication.* Thousand Oaks, CA: Sage.

Harrison, K. (n.d.). Communicating during a crisis. *Cutting Edge PR*. Retrieved from http://www.cuttingedgepr.com/articles/crisiscomm_comm_during.asp

Kwansah-Aidoo, K., & George, A. M. (2017). Communication, culture and crisis in a transboundary context. In A. George, & K. Kwansah-Aidoo (Eds.), *Culture and crisis communication* (pp. 3–18). Hoboken, NJ: Wiley.

Lachlan, K. A., Spence, P., & Lin, X. (2018). Natural disasters, Twitter and stakeholder communication. In L. Austin, & Y. Jin (Eds.), *Social media and crisis communication* (pp. 296–303). New York, NY: Routledge.

Lewis, C. S. (1985). *First and second things*. Glasgow, Scotland: William Collins Sons (Original work published in 1942).

Liska, C., Petrun, E. L., Sellnow, T. L., & Seeger, M. W. (2012). Chaos theory, self-organization and industrial accidents: Crisis communication. *Southern Communication Journal, 77*(3), 180–197.

Littlefield, R. S. (2013). Communicating risk and crisis communication to multiple publics. In A. J. DuBrin (Ed.), *Handbook of research on crisis leadership in organizations* (pp. 231–251). Northampton, MA: Edward Elgar Publishing.

Lu, H., & Schuldt, J. P. (2016). Compassion for climate change victims and support for mitigation policy. *Journal of Environmental Psychology, 45*, 192–200.

North, M., Li, C., Liu, J., & Ji, Y. G. (2018). Using Twitter for crisis communication: A content analysis of Fortune 500 companies. In L. Austin, & Y. Jin (Eds.), *Social media and crisis communication* (pp. 197–208). New York, NY: Routledge.

Phillips, B. (2013, August 27). The spokesperson you choose speaks volumes. *My PRSA*. Retrieved from http://apps.prsa.org/Intelligence/Tactics/Articles/view/10320/1082/The_spokesperson_you_choose_speaks_volumes#.WiQ9gTeIaUk

Reuters. (2010, June 10) BP CEO apologizes for "thoughtless" oil spill comment. Retrieved from https://www.reuters.com/article/us-oil-spill-bp-apology/bp-ceo-apologizes-for-thoughtless-oil-spill-comment-idUSTRE6515NQ20100602

Sellnow, T. L., Sellnow, D. D., Lane, D. R., & Littlefield, R. S. (2012). The value of instructional communication in crisis situations: Restoring order to chaos. *Risk Analysis, 32*(4), 633–643.

Sellnow, T. L., Ulmer, R. R., & Snider, M. (1998). The compatibility of corrective action in organizational crisis communication. *Communication Quarterly, 46*, 60–74.

Simpson, A. V., Clegg, S., & Pinae Cunha, M. (2013). Expressing compassion in the face of crisis: Organizational practices in the aftermath of the Brisbane floods of 2011. *Journal of Contingencies and Crisis Management, 21*(2), 115–124.

Tennessee: Community awaits answers. (2009, January 4). *Times Free Press.* Retrieved from http://www.timesfreepress.com/news/news/story/2009/jan/04/tennessee-community-awaits-answers/202365

Ulmer, R. R., Sellnow, T. L., & Seeger, M. W. (2017). *Effective crisis communication: Moving from crisis to opportunity.* Thousand Oaks, CA: Sage Publications.

Witte, B. (2002, January 17). Train derailment kills one, sends ammonia cloud over Minot. *Bismarck Tribune.* Retrieved from http://bismarcktribune.com/uncategorized/train-derailment-kills-one-sends-ammonia-cloud-over-minot/article_35ad8aeb-21a9-5be6-8c98-543ba8b71471.html

10

Uncertainty

Accept Uncertainty and Ambiguity

As we discussed in the introduction, uncertainty is a natural element of crises and crisis communication. Crises and disasters are by definition abnormal, unpredictable, and uncertain events. Many crises occur as surprises, thereby requiring time to assess what has happened, why it has happened, and what steps to take to address the impending damage or threat. Other crises, such as hurricanes, are predictable, but the actual course they will follow and their intensity when making landfall are all uncertain. Accordingly, a best practice of crisis communication is to acknowledge the uncertainty and ambiguity inherent in a crisis situation.

Despite the uncertainty inherent in crises, crisis spokespersons often feel a need to be overly certain and overly reassuring in their messages to publics. This intuitive urge may be largely a consequence of a belief that publics cannot accept uncertainty in situations and need certainty in the face of a crisis, even when information is simply unavailable. Unfortunately, overly reassuring statements in the face of an uncertain and equivocal situation may reduce a spokesperson's credibility. This potential for diminished credibility is particularly high when crises evolve in startling, unpredictable ways.

What Causes Uncertainty for Publics?

Uncertainty occurs when we have difficulty drawing conclusions from the available information. This means we can't predict what will happen. The discomfort of this uncertainty increases for individuals who are closest in proximity to the crisis (Spence et al., 2005). Specifically, uncertainty makes comprehension difficult when the available information is insufficient, multifaceted, or doubted (Brashers, 2001). Recognizing these

Communication in Times of Trouble: Best Practices for Crisis and Emergency Risk Communication, First Edition. Matthew W. Seeger and Timothy L. Sellnow.
© 2019 John Wiley & Sons, Inc. Published 2019 by John Wiley & Sons, Inc.

three signs of uncertainty enables crisis spokespersons to both acknowledge and take steps toward resolving the resulting confusion and frustration experienced by publics. We discuss these three features of uncertainty in the following paragraphs.

When information about a crisis is insufficient, we mean it is either "unavailable or inconsistent" (Brashers, 2001, p. 478). Crises typically instill shock for individuals on multiple levels, including those tasked with responding to, those affected by, and those observing the situation. For example, when a downtown Minneapolis, Minn., bridge on I-35W collapsed into the Mississippi River during rush hour, the community was both horrified and confused. Because the bridge was on a commonly used route, residents were at once concerned about the victims of the crisis and uncertain about how to navigate their way through the city. In response to this uncertainty, Nelson, Spence, and Lachlan (2009) observed that many residents in the area turned to live media coverage of the event to resolve their uncertainty. In this case, local media kept residents informed of the deaths, injuries, rescues, and damage while also suggesting alternate transportation routes.

Information is multifaceted when it is "ambiguous, complex, unpredictable, or probabilistic" (Brashers, 2001, p. 478). Weick (1995) explains that ambiguous information is particularly frustrating for publics. He sees ambiguity as "an ongoing stream that supports several different interpretations at the same time" (pp. 91–92). Crisis situations with prolonged waiting periods such as hurricanes often create such ambiguity. For example, Hurricane Matthew created considerable consternation for residents along the east coast of Florida in 2016. Some predictions had the hurricane hitting the coast at full strength. As the hurricane came closer to landfall, the projections showed a lesser likelihood the hurricane would maintain its current strength or direction. Yet messages from Florida's governor continued to warn residents of extreme danger. In the end, Hurricane Matthew produced little damage in Florida but did cause considerable flooding in states further north. The drastically different interpretations of the available evidence for Hurricane Matthew created ambiguity for residents that many resented after the hurricane passed by.

Information is doubted "when people feel insecure in their own state of knowledge or the state of knowledge in general" (Brashers, 2001, p. 478). Publics often feel doubt about the available information in response to politically motivated acts of violence. For example, almost half of Americans participating in a 2016 Pew Research Center poll still worried that the government's antiterrorism policies had not done enough since 9/11 to protect the United States (Pew Research Center, 2016). Lingering concerns and doubts about the ability to defend against politically motivated acts of violence are intentional. For such acts to produce political or policy influence they must "inculcate fear" (Tuman, 2003, p. 7). Consequently, such acts are typically done seemingly at random without a clear focus on who will be victimized. The resulting uncertainty in this case, then, is the means by which anxiety is nurtured.

How Do Publics Respond to Uncertainty?

In their most severe forms, crises instill a sense of uncertainty that Weick (1993) characterizes as a cosmology episode. Cosmology episodes occur when, in response to crises, people suddenly and profoundly feel that the order they once assumed in the universe no longer exists. Those experiencing a cosmology episode are so traumatized they momentarily cannot make sense of what is happening around them. Such incidents are devastating because both the ability to comprehend what is occurring and the means to rebuild that level of comprehension collapse together. Weick summarizes the human reaction to cosmology episodes in three statements:

- I have never been here before,
- I have no idea where I am,
- and I have no idea who can help me (pp. 634–635).

Imagine, for example, the initial reaction of motorists either on or approaching the Minneapolis bridge as it collapsed into the Mississippi River. The thought of an eight-lane bridge in the middle of a major city collapsing had not likely crossed the minds of these individuals. Those whose cars were stranded on the bridge likely wondered what was happening and whether or how they could be rescued. One of the surgeons who operated on injured drivers and passengers described his patients by saying, "They were in shock, they were happy to be alive, but they felt sad for all the people they had seen" (Levy, 2007, para. 9).

In the end, 13 people lost their lives on the bridge the day it collapsed and 145 were injured (Ferraro & Clarey, 2012). The bridge collapse also created a larger crisis of confidence in the city's infrastructure for residents. As Weick (1995) explains, "people frequently see things differently when they are shocked into attention, whether the shock is one of necessity, opportunity, or threat" (pp. 84–85). The shock of the bridge collapse created a sense of urgency that inspired inspections of transportation infrastructure in Minnesota and across the country. The Minneapolis bridge was rebuilt with added safety features and Minnesota intensified the assessment and repair of its bridges. To do so, Minnesota undertook a 10-year initiative to repair all bridges with observed problems. Minnesota's state bridge engineer described the results of the bridge safety initiative, saying, "Certainly we've done a lot to ensure the safety of bridges so it doesn't happen again, so I feel confident about the advancements we've made in bridge design, construction, inspection, maintenance and that all works toward good bridge safety" (Schaper, 2017, para. 16). Ultimately, this initiative sought to replace the uncertainty Minnesotans felt about the safety of their bridges with confidence that far-reaching and long-term improvements had been made.

What Kind of Information Do Publics Seek to Reduce Their Uncertainty?

Uncertainty is an uncomfortable state creating a drive for uncertainty reduction, usually by seeking more information (Berger, 1987). As publics seek to reduce uncertainty, they initially pursue information about what actions they can take to protect themselves. We discuss the importance and nature of messages that empower publics to protect themselves in the following section. In addition to empowerment in the face of crises, publics also frequently ask questions seeking to resolve multiple interpretations of evidence, the intent behind the actions preceding the crisis, and the assignment of responsibility (Ulmer & Sellnow, 2000).

Early in crises, there is limited evidence available about the cause of the crisis. As investigations are conducted, evidence explaining what happened can reduce uncertainty for publics. Conversely, competing interpretations of this evidence can create a degree of ambiguity that actually heightens uncertainty. For example, British Petroleum's (BP) 2010 tragic Deepwater Horizon oil spill in the Gulf of Mexico caused tremendous damage that was readily observable by publics. As of 2018, the company is still engaged in a massive cleanup effort projected to cost tens of billions of dollars. Although the well-being of wildlife and the surface appearance of the Gulf have improved notably, "scientists debate just how much oil from Deepwater Horizon is still out in the environment" (Ferris, 2017, para. 15). Much of the oil was degraded by naturally occurring microbes below the ocean's surface. How much oil remains and the potential for this oil to cause long-term environmental damage are still contested. Complex evidence, in this case technical measures of oil residue on the ocean floor, often create ambiguity because of competing interpretations of the same findings. As such, this kind of scientific discussion can actually increase postcrisis uncertainty for both decision makers and their publics.

Questions of intent focus on the motives and planning process that occurred prior to the crisis. Answering questions of intent can, for example, explain whether the crisis was caused by an accident or malfeasance.

If an organization had good intentions prior to the crisis and the events are seen as purely accidental, publics tend to be more sympathetic. If, however, the organization was motivated by profit, thereby causing the organization to cut corners in its crisis planning or safety measures, publics are much less forgiving (Coombs, 2015). As the investigation into the Gulf crisis unfolded, BP was plagued by accusations that, for the sake of profit, the company failed to engage in adequate safety measures before beginning to drill at extreme depths in the Gulf. BP was even portrayed in the feature film *Deepwater Horizon* as prioritizing profit over safety. The movie grossed over $100 million (Deepwater Horizon, 2016). The pressing question for publics as they watched oil gushing into the Gulf day after day from the vantage point of an underwater camera was, "How could this happen?" In this case, BP's intentions have been consistently portrayed as impure. BP provided a rebuttal to the accusations that their intentions were self-serving, but public opinion has largely rejected these counterarguments.

Questions of responsibility involve assigning blame for the crisis. Assigning blame can reduce uncertainty for publics by identifying a source that is accountable for corrective action and liable for compensating those harmed. With natural disasters, responsibility is often interpreted as an act of God. By contrast, for industrial accidents and similar crises, responsibility is typically assigned to an organization or organizations. Because this responsibility carries with it a significant legal and financial toll, the assignment of blame is often debated in both public discussion and the courtroom. For example, BP and Transocean, BP's contractor that actually performed the drilling in the Gulf, initially blamed each other for the crisis. BP accepted its responsibility for the cleanup but insisted the failures in the technology in place to prevent the type of blowout that occurred in the Deepwater Horizon were the fault of Transocean. Transocean countered that BP oversaw another contractor, Halliburton, that had failed to adequately create a cement plug that was essential in preventing the crisis (Quinn, 2010). Such debates over responsibility do little to reassure publics the crisis will be resolved. As we mentioned previously, focusing on legal and reputational matters while people are disoriented and suffering in the wake of a crisis shows a lack of compassion.

How Can Organizations Avoid Overreassuring Their Publics?

When responding to the fear or outrage of publics, organizations may be tempted to overreassure their stakeholders. Ulmer and Pyle (2016) explain, "organizations that are focused on protecting their image most often use communication strategies to absolve themselves from blame, minimize the crisis, or over-reassure the public about the impact of the crisis" (p. 114). To do so, organizations often manipulate or withhold information. In the short term, overreassuring audiences can create a momentary calming effect. In the long term, however, Ulmer and Pyle explain that overreassuring audiences deprives the organization of the credibility it urgently needs to communicate effectively in postcrisis phase. As we explained previously, being open and honest at all phases of a crisis helps organizations maintain their credibility—even if doing so causes initial damage to the organization's reputation.

We acknowledge overreassurance may also be intertwined with the uncertainty surrounding the crisis. Spokespersons may minimize the perceived impact of a crisis because they sincerely believe the risk is minimal or perhaps nonexistent. For example, when Thomas Eric Duncan was diagnosed in a Dallas hospital as having contracted the Ebola virus, Tom Frieden, then-director of the Centers for Disease Control and Prevention (CDC), said, "I have no doubt that we'll stop this in its tracks in the U.S." (Muskal, 2014, para. 2). Not long after making this comment, two nurses who had treated Duncan were diagnosed with Ebola. This news of Ebola having spread within the hospital caused public confidence in the CDC's ability to contain the disease to plummet. Indeed, Frieden's comments, seen as overreassurance, haunted him throughout the crisis. Frieden said what he believed at the time. Had he tempered his initial comments by accepting the risk of the disease spreading, Frieden likely would have created considerable alarm. Yet, having to backtrack on what was perceived as overreassurance hampered his credibility for the remainder of the crisis. The lesson from this case is that caution in reassuring statements early in the crisis may cause short-term challenges, but such restraint can help spokespersons avoid long-term credibility problems.

What Are Some Other Ways to Manage Uncertainty?

A best practice of crisis communication, then, is to acknowledge the uncertainty inherent in the crisis situation with statements such as, "The situation is fluid" and "We do not yet have all the facts." As we discussed earlier, this form of ambiguity is strategic in that it allows the communicator to refine the message as more information becomes available and to avoid statements likely to be shown as inaccurate as more information is obtained. Many of the best practices will help manage and reduce uncertainty. For example, having a precrisis plan helps people know what to do during a crisis. Preevent relationships with stakeholders can help crisis managers predict responses. Maintaining open relationships with publics and the media will increase the flow of information.

Karl Weick's extensive work on sensemaking during crises provides a useful framework for maintaining flexible communication that acknowledges uncertainty during crises. Foremost for Weick (1988) is the need for organizations to willingly let go of their previous assumptions once a crisis occurs. Weick explains that organizational leaders often provide tenacious justifications that their previous assumptions and planning can minimize the crisis. Unfortunately, these assumptions are often proven false. Frieden's insistence in absolute terms that the Ebola virus would not spread within the Dallas hospital is an example of a tenacious justification for existing plans. Many spokespersons engage in tenacious justification or rigidity in their crisis response because, like Frieden, they assume certainty where it does not exist. Avoiding statements with such certainty is strongly advised.

To fully engage in sensemaking, spokespersons should recognize that crisis communication is a process of uncertainty reduction. This process transpires progressively in the crisis and postcrisis phases, continuing into the return to a new precrisis phase. The ongoing discovery and clarification of information require steady adaptation and constant communication. Weick's (1995) explanation of the sensemaking process can be summarized in four general strategies for crisis spokespersons: let go of previous assumptions, take action, collect feedback, and retain the lessons taught by the crisis.

First, uncertainty reduction is based on letting go of assumptions that can blind the organization to the true nature of the crisis. In many cases, the flawed assumptions made by an organization result in missed opportunities to prevent crises or, once a crisis occurs, limit the capacity for the organization to respond. Weick (1995) explains that organizations must first move beyond tenacious justifications of previous assumptions and prepare to take whatever novel actions may be needed to manage the crisis.

The uncertainty or ambiguity created by the crisis should not preempt the organization from taking action. Enacting a reasonable strategy to address the needs of the organization's stakeholders is essential. Central to this enactment process is understanding how the organization's previous actions contributed or may have contributed to the crisis (Weick, 2001). From the sensemaking perspective, then, the first step is to stop doing more of the wrong thing. This step is accomplished through a thorough and frank assessment of how previous assumptions and actions may have caused the crisis or diminished the organization's readiness to respond. Recognizing these failures and replacing them with novel actions is essential to uncertainty reduction.

Once an organization reconsiders its previous actions, the major objective is obtaining as much feedback as quickly as possible about the effectiveness or ineffectiveness of whatever alternate strategies the organization has enacted. Feedback from publics is essential in this step of the sensemaking process. Weick (2001) explains, "Managers literally must wade into the ocean of events that surround the organization and actively try to make sense of them" (p. 244). For Weick, this process involves gathering as much data as possible, interpreting the information, and deriving lessons learned. These lessons enable organizations to select the best-known actions for preventing or responding to crises.

Based on feedback obtained and the interpretation of it, organizations retain these lessons learned about the most effective strategies for crisis management. The retention of these lessons contributes to organizational memory and learning. The goal is that these strategies will be retained and influence the organization's precrisis planning and continuous environmental scanning of risk issues. Thus, retention of lessons learned allows the uncertainty reduction process to come full circle from crisis to postcrisis assessment and back to precrisis planning. These lessons provide "cause maps" that heighten organizations' sensitivity to small failures that, if acknowledged, could prevent future crises (Weick, 2001, p. 305).

In summary, spokespersons can manage uncertainty through four steps of sensemaking:

1) Accept uncertainty by letting go of previous assumptions and preparing to address the novel aspects of the crisis.
2) Take reasonable actions that prioritize the needs of stakeholders over concerns for the organization's reputation.
3) Constantly seek feedback on the success or failure of the initial actions and be prepared to enact alternative solutions.
4) Retain the lessons learned about how to best respond to similar crises and include these lessons in precrisis planning.

By acknowledging failure, taking reasonable actions in response to these failures, carefully scrutinizing these actions, and deriving lessons learned from the crisis, an organization can both reduce uncertainty about the current crisis and avoid repeating similar mistakes in the future.

What Are the Ethical Standards for Managing Uncertainty?

Ideally, organizations seek to reduce uncertainty as soon as possible after a crisis begins and to quickly share what is known with all stakeholders. Doing so enables stakeholders to make informed decisions about protecting themselves and about the organization's effectiveness in responding to the crisis. Conversely, organizations can engage in the unethical practice of strategically increasing ambiguity through the manipulation of information and, in so doing, deflect responsibility or criticism for the crisis. As we have discussed, information related to crises is often ambiguous. From an ethical perspective, however, we set forth the following distinction:

1) Strategic ambiguity is ethical when it contributes to the complete understanding of an issue by posing alternative views based on complete and unbiased data that aim to inform.
2) Strategic ambiguity is unethical if it poses alternative interpretations using biased and/or incomplete information that aims to deceive (Ulmer & Sellnow, 1997, p. 217).

The ongoing discussion about BP's cleanup process in response to the Deep Horizon crisis is a fitting example. Claims that much of the oil is being consumed by natural microbes are ethical if such claims are based on the best science and the best evidence available. Such claims could, however, be unethical if they are made in an attempt to relieve the company of its responsibility simply because much of the oil is difficult to find in the vast Gulf of Mexico. We base this distinction on Nilsen's (1974) ethic of significant choice.

Nilsen (1974) argues that free and informed choice is essential to any democracy. Therefore, publics cannot exercise their full freedom when making significant choices that may profoundly affect their lives unless they have "the best information available when the decision must be made" (p. 45). Nilsen accepts the whole truth cannot be known through human interaction. In addition to the uncertainty caused by crises, some degree of bias or ambiguity is always present. However, he maintains "there should be no less information provided, no less rigor of reasoning communicated, and no less democratic spirit fostered than circumstances make feasible" (p. 73). When organizations seek to mislead publics by denying them access to information or by misrepresenting the information that is known, they are violating the ethic of significant choice.

Returning to our earlier example, after the Minneapolis bridge collapse, Minnesota's legislature was forthright in sharing information about all bridges in the state known to have structural damages. One state legislator acknowledged that, before the collapse, Minnesotans had a "general sense" that bridges in the state were deteriorating, but they did not comprehend "the scale of the problem" (Montgomery, 2017, para. 7). The transparency of Minnesota's legislature in discussing the dangers posed by other bridges in the state helped generate support for a higher gas tax, much of which was devoted to repairing and replacing problematic bridges. In the end, "Minnesota not only replaced the collapsed bridge, but also made a concerted effort to repair and replace hundreds of other bridges around the state" (Montgomery, 2017, para. 2). The open communication and public involvement evident in Minnesota's response to its bridge infrastructure needs clearly meet the criteria of Nilsen's (1974) ethic of significant choice.

Summary

By their nature, crises and disasters are abnormal, unpredictable, and uncertain events. Thus, spokespersons are advised to accept this uncertainty and to avoid overly certain and overly reassuring statements. Eventually, the errors prevalent in such overstatements typically reduce a spokesperson's credibility. Alternatively, spokespersons should make statements that reflect the fluidity of the information available. Maintaining the types of relationships advised in the third and sixth best practices can help create a flow of information that accommodates this degree of uncertainty.

Key Takeaways for Accepting Uncertainty and Ambiguity

1) Crises are always highly ambiguous and uncertain events and this is one of the reasons communication is so important. Organizations must accept the uncertainty that comes with a crisis and plan for managing the crisis by providing appropriate information.
2) Uncertainty is stressful and stakeholders will actively seek out information to address specific needs during a crisis and to reduce their overall uncertainty about what is happening and what they should do.
3) Stakeholders will seek out information from a variety of sources—including friends and family, government officials, and community leaders—and through a variety of channels, including face to face, social media, and legacy media. If official sources of information are unavailable or do not provide adequate information, stakeholders will turn to unofficial sources. This can result in conflicting messages and confusion.
4) Making sense of what is happening during a crisis is necessary to manage and reduce uncertainty. Sensemaking requires letting go of assumptions, setting priorities, seeking feedback, and retaining and applying lessons learned.
5) Although a temptation to overreassure publics often occurs during a crisis, doing so can actually create additional uncertainty by reducing credibility. Acknowledging the uncertainty inherent in a crisis situation is both more accurate and more responsible.

References

Berger, C. R. (1987). Communicating under uncertainty. In M. E. Roloff, & G. R. Miller (Eds.), *Interpersonal processes: New directions for communication research* (pp. 39–62). Newbury Park, CA: Sage.

Brashers, D. E. (2001). Communication and uncertainty management. *Journal of Communication, 51,* 477–497.

Coombs, W. T. (2015). *Ongoing crisis communication: Planning, managing, and responding* (4th ed.). Thousand Oaks, CA: Sage.

Deepwater Horizon. (2016). *Box Office Mojo.* Retrieved from http://www.boxofficemojo.com/movies/?id=deepwaterhorizon.htm

Ferraro, N., & Clarey, J. (2012, July 30). I-35 bridge collapse: Five stories, five years later. *Pioneer Press.* Retrieved from http://www.twincities.com/2012/07/30/i-35w-bridge-collapse-five-stories-five-years-later

Ferris, R. (2017, June 26). Much of the Deepwater Horizon oil spill has disappeared because of bacteria. *CNBC.* Retrieved from https://www.cnbc.com/2017/06/26/much-of-the-deepwater-horizon-oil-spill-has-disappeared-because-of-bacteria.html

Levy, P. (2007, November 29). 4 dead, 79 injured, 20 missing after dozens of vehicles plummet into river. *StarTribune.* Retrieved from http://www.startribune.com/4-dead-79-injured-20-missing-after-dozens-of-vehicles-plummet-into-river/11593606

Montgomery, D. (2017, July 30). Many bridges found deficient after I-35W collapse. Here's how Minnesota responded. *Twin Cities Pioneer Press.* Retrieved from https://www.twincities.com/2017/07/30/after-collapse-minnesota-fixed-deficient-bridges

Muskal, M. (2014, October 16). Four Ebola quotes that may come back to haunt CDC's Tom Frieden. *Los Angeles Times.* Retrieved from http://www.latimes.com/nation/nationnow/la-na-four-ebola-quotes-haunt-frieden-20141016-story.html

Nelson, L. D., Spence, P. R., & Lachlan, K. A. (2009). Learning from the media in the aftermath of a crisis: Findings from the Minneapolis bridge collapse. *Electronic News, 3*(4), 176–192.

Nilsen, T. R. (1974). *Ethics of speech communication* (2nd ed.). Indianapolis, IN: Bobbs-Merrill Company.

Pew Research Center. (2016, September 7). 15 years after 911, a sharp partisan divide on ability of terrorists to strike U.S. Retrieved from http://www.people-press.org/2016/09/07/15-years-after-911-a-sharp-partisan-divide-on-ability-of-terrorists-to-strike-u-s

Quinn, J. (2010, May 11). BP and Transocean blame each other for Gulf of Mexico oil spill. *The Telegraph.* Retrieved from http://www.telegraph.co.uk/finance/newsbysector/energy/oilandgas/7712652/BP-and-Transocean-blame-each-other-for-Gulf-of-Mexico-oil-spill.html

Schaper, D. (2017). 10 years after bridge collapse, America is still crumbling. *National Public Radio*. Retrieved from https://www.npr.org/2017/08/01/ 540669701/10-years-after-bridge-collapse-america-is-still-crumbling

Spence, P. R., Westerman, D., Skalski, P. D., Seeger, M., Ulmer, R. R., Venette, S., & Sellnow, T. L. (2005). Proxemic effects on information seeking after the September 11 attacks. *Communication Research Reports, 22*(1), 39–46.

Tuman, J. S. (2003). *Communicating terror: The rhetorical dimensions of terrorism*. Thousand Oaks, CA: Sage.

Ulmer, R. R., & Pyle, A. S. (2016). International organizational crisis communication: A simple rules approach to managing crisis complexity. In A. Schwarz, M. W. Seeger, & C. Auer (Eds.), *The handbook of international crisis communication research* (pp. 108–118). Malden, MA: Wiley Blackwell.

Ulmer, R. R., & Sellnow, T. L. (1997). Strategic ambiguity and the ethic of significant choice. *Communication Studies, 48*, 215–233.

Ulmer, R. R., & Sellnow, T. L. (2000). Consistent questions of ambiguity: Jack in the box as a case study. *Journal of Business Ethics, 25*, 143–155.

Weick, K. E. (1988). Enacted sensemaking in crisis situations. *Journal of Management Studies, 25*, 305–317.

Weick, K. E. (1993). The collapse of sensemaking in organizations: The Mann Gulch disaster. *Administrative Science Quarterly, 38*, 628–652.

Weick, K. E. (1995). *Sensemaking in organizations*. Thousand Oaks, CA: Sage.

Weick, K. E. (2001). *Making sense of the organization*. Malden, MA: Blackwell Business.

11

Empowerment

Communicate Messages of Empowerment

The ultimate form of empowerment for publics is to receive information advising them on what actions they can take to protect themselves, their loved ones, and their property. During a crisis, be it a product recall or a hurricane, people want to know what they can do to reduce their risk or offset the harm they experience or could experience. They also want to understand what is happening and why. As such, a best practice of crisis communication is to tell the public what is happening and instruct them on the appropriate actions they can take for self-protection or community protection.

How Can Messages Empower Publics?

One of the impacts of a crisis is the perceived loss of control. People affected by a crisis often feel things are being done to them and that they have lost their ability to comprehend and control their own destiny. As we explained previously, Weick (1993) designates this consistent emotional response as a cosmology episode. At this point in the lives of publics engulfed in crisis, they are experiencing something at an extreme that is new to them and they do not fully understand what is happening or know where they can turn for help. Communicating recommended actions for self-protection can help reduce these feelings of confusion, impending doom, and helplessness by recreating some sense of control.

Based on the nature of the specific crisis event, these messages will vary widely. In the case of natural disasters or chemical spills, the messages may include recommendations for evacuating or sheltering in place. During epidemics or pandemics, recommendations will likely explain how to obtain vaccinations for individuals and their families, ensure appropriate hygiene, limit public interaction, monitor particular

Communication in Times of Trouble: Best Practices for Crisis and Emergency Risk Communication, First Edition. Matthew W. Seeger and Timothy L. Sellnow.
© 2019 John Wiley & Sons, Inc. Published 2019 by John Wiley & Sons, Inc.

symptoms, and receive treatment if infected. During food recalls or water contamination events, recommendations focus on avoiding particular kinds of foods or food products, preparing food, strategies for making available water fit for drinking, or where to obtain safe food and water. In most cases, self-protection may be as simple as encouraging stakeholders to monitor both new and legacy media sources for additional developments. In other cases, publics receive information from first responders entering their communities with supplies and protective advice.

Another set of recommended actions involve community or group activities. During the Zika outbreak in Puerto Rico, a recommended action was to reduce the amount of standing water throughout the community. This required people who were not necessarily at risk to take actions to help protect others who would be affected. Activities like working on sandbag crews during flooding or working with others to remove debris from roads following storms are community-based actions that can help reduce harm.

What Are the Components of an Empowering Message?

The specific action recommended must match the specifics of the situation. Messages of empowerment are most effective when they have specific characteristics: information that helps the audience internalize the risk; a distribution of consistent messages through channels that are available to the audiences at risk; an explanation of the crisis at hand; and specific, tangible actions publics can take to protect themselves, their loved ones, and their property (Mileti & Peek, 2000; Sellnow, Lane, Sellnow, & Littlefield, 2017). A mnemonic device or prompt for recalling these four components is IDEA: internalization, distribution, explanation, and action (Sellnow & Sellnow, 2013). We describe each of these components in our answers to the following questions.

How Can Risk and Crisis Communicators Help Their Publics *Internalize* the Risk?

Internalization involves identifying the key audiences and convincing them to attend to the message. The goal is to help the audiences understand the level of threat they are facing, either directly or indirectly. Direct threats involve immediate risks to individuals, their loved ones, or their assets. Hurricanes, for example, take days to develop, allowing specialists to collect data, make forecasts, and share these forecasts with local meteorologists. These meteorologists, along with national weather broadcasters, then share the developing risks with audiences. In this case, individuals can see the direction of the storm and make decisions about evacuating or sheltering in place. In other instances, such as tornadoes, flash floods, or wildfires, there is less time to explain the emerging risk to a community. In these cases, internalization of the risk is possible only through short-term weather forecasts of droughts or heavy rainfall. Residents living in or visiting low-lying areas or those living in hot, dry areas surrounded by flammable vegetation can also be alerted to their heightened risk before and during rainy and dry seasons. The key to internalization is finding those who are at heightened risk and designing messages specifically for them. When risk and crisis communicators can tailor their messages to show individuals their specific risk of harm due to an emerging threat, they are more likely to take an interest in the message and to respond accordingly (Sellnow, Sellnow, Lane, & Littlefield, 2012).

Publics can also internalize a risk and crisis message indirectly. Many people feel a natural impulse to help those facing tragedy. This compulsion, referred to as humanism, is rooted in the philosophical standpoint and prioritizes the uniqueness and unconditional worth of human beings (Ulmer, Sellnow, & Seeger, 2017). This humanistic regard reaches far beyond our immediate communities. Concerned observers donated millions of dollars to the Red Cross and other agencies after tragedies such as the 2010 Haiti earthquake and the tsunami caused by an earthquake in the Indian Ocean in December 2004. In some cases, the money exceeded the expectations of these agencies. When those seeking to raise funds for disaster relief tap into the humanistic compulsion to help people in need, they are creating opportunities for those observing the crisis to internalize the event and participate vicariously in the recovery effort. Indirect internalization also occurs through the memorialization process. Memorials of past crises provide solace for those who directly experienced the crisis, but they also invite those who were not directly involved and future generations to internalize the lessons learned from the disaster. For example, the Oklahoma City Memorial honors each of the victims but also teaches lessons about alternatives to violence (Veil, Sellnow, & Heald, 2011). Such lessons are fitting given the 1995 crisis was the result of a domestic terrorist attack. American citizens Timothy McVeigh and Terry Nichols created and detonated a bomb outside the Murrah Federal Building in downtown Oklahoma City. The attack killed 168 people and injured 680 more.

How Should Messages Be *Distributed* to Publics?

The ever-shifting landscape of communication technology has created many new opportunities for distributing risk and crisis messages. Specifically, advancing technology has made targeting messages to those at the highest risk much easier and faster than in the past. For example, many government agencies such as the Food and Drug Administration (FDA), Centers for Disease Control and Prevention (CDC), and United States Department of Agriculture (USDA) have established public networks through social media. Individuals can voluntarily opt into or join these networks, allowing these agencies to tailor messages for specific subgroups who are at risk. For example, the United States Geological Survey (USGS) has created an earthquake early warning program via the Internet that residents in southern California can subscribe to. Strong shaking moves outward from the point where an earthquake begins. Residents who use the USGS's warning system can receive an alert letting them know an earthquake has started near them. The shaking travels quickly, giving residents only a matter of seconds to respond. Still, knowing the shaking is about to begin gives those who subscribe to the system an opportunity to quickly move away from the most dangerous areas of a room and take cover under a table, desk, or other surface. Automobile manufacturers regularly keep records of those who have purchased their vehicles, allowing them to send recall notices. Some grocery store chains provide club cards that both provide discounts and collect data on what each shopper purchases. In some cases, consumers can opt into programs that allow the store to warn them if the store's records indicate the consumer has purchased a product that has been recalled because of a food safety threat. These examples demonstrate how social media and smartphones have greatly advanced the capacity for risk and crisis communicators to establish networks before or during crises to provide tailored messages for those in harm's way (Sellnow et al., 2012).

Another advantage provided by emerging media is the increased personal networking capacity of warning messages. Prior to social media, individuals shared warning messages in face-to-face interactions or by telephone. Although these message exchanges worked well in neighborhoods or work settings, their reach is dwarfed by the capacity for messages to spread through personal social media networks. In addition to joining networks sponsored by organizations and agencies, publics can follow a variety of individuals in their communities via social media outlets such as Twitter or Facebook. Within seconds, warning messages can span throughout an entire community. Of course, face-to-face interaction is still extremely compelling for crisis communicators. New media, however, has increased the accessibility and influence of crisis communication via social media (Jin, Liu, & Austin, 2014).

How Much *Explanation* of the Crisis Is Necessary?

Explanation refers to those messages intended to give publics an understanding of what is happening, what caused the crisis, and how the crisis can or will be abated. Meeting the expectations of publics for explanation, however, is seemingly paradoxical. As we discussed previously, those at risk want information immediately that may or may not be known. Equally challenging is the seemingly paradoxical desire of publics to have explanations of highly complex information delivered to them on a level that is both brief and easily comprehensible by nonscientists.

Unfortunately, subject matter experts often fail to meet their audiences' expectation to see complex information delivered simply and meaningfully (Arlikatti, Lindell, & Prater, 2007). Although this shortfall is understandable, given the paradoxical nature of the demand, there are opportunities for improvement. When researchers conduct analyses of content delivered by subject matter experts, they often find the scientific explanation of the crisis occupies by far the most space (Frisby, Veil, & Sellnow, 2014). This emphasis on explanation may be fitting for a subject matter expert's peers or for audiences indirectly affected by the crisis. For those struggling to deal with the crisis, however, the information is perceived as excessive, burdensome, and largely irrelevant to their immediate needs (Frisby et al., 2014).

The difficulty of adapting scientific information into simple terms is understandable. Scientists on every level work under the expectation of peer review. Scientific research is conducted, summarized in written form, presented for blind review to peers, critiqued, and eventually deemed either credible or unreliable. This peer review process can and often does take months to years to complete. The urgency and short response time of crises force subject matter experts to suspend their normal expectations for peer review and to provide explanations immediately. How can subject matter experts resolve this paradox of presenting the complex simply? The answer is to carefully analyze the audience members and determine their immediate needs.

For example, the porcine epidemic diarrhea virus (PEDV) ravaged the swine industry in 2013 and 2014, killing as many as 100,000 piglets and young hogs per week (Strom, 2014). Producers were emotionally and financially devastated by the disease as it spread rapidly throughout the United States. Unfortunately, little was known about PEDV at the time. The disease was likely introduced to the United States through the purchase of grain or animals from other countries. Without an existing protocol for diagnosing, treating, and avoiding the spread of the disease, the swine industry scrambled to fill the information void. Filling this void required the unified efforts of the National Pork Board, the National Pork Producers Council, the American Association of Swine Veterinarians, extension agents, local veterinarians, and other swine specialists. These agencies collaborated to conduct research and translate and distribute their recommendations to practicing veterinarians and producers. This collaborative undertaking resulted in the creation of a fitting explanation of the disease with unprecedented expediency. Producers asked for short, succinct, easy-to-read messages they could quickly process. Understanding why their animals were dying, how the disease was spreading, and the potential for a vaccine was knowledge highly valued by producers. Producers did not, however, want an extensive medical explanation requiring valuable time to decipher—time needed for attending to their sick and dying animals.

In cases such as PEDV that are dominated by uncertainty, the best explanations follow four sequential steps:

1) This is what we know now.
2) This is what we do not know.
3) This is what we are doing to find out what we do not know.
4) This is when we will communicate publicly again.

These steps, as we discussed previously, are also fitting for slow-moving crises with high uncertainty such as hurricanes. Determining where and when hurricanes will make landfall is always a work in progress. Even when hurricanes do make landfall, they can rotate and advance in ways that are unpredictable until a shift in direction begins. Thus, frequent updates of the explanation process are needed. Once a general understanding of who or what is in danger and why is known, specific recommendations for self-protective actions are needed.

How Should Recommendations for Self-Protective *Actions* Be Communicated?

The advice airlines give before every flight may seem mundane to frequent fliers, but these action steps provide passengers a degree of reassurance that, if a crisis arises, there are steps they can take to enhance their chances of survival. This form of empowerment, referred to as self-efficacy, often reduces some of the stress publics experience before undertaking activities that involve a degree of risk (Sellnow et al., 2012). To be effective, however, publics must believe they have both the knowledge and physical ability needed to perform the protective actions and that the recommended actions could indeed reduce their risk (Bandura, 1982). Fitting an oxygen mask to one's face and efficiently exiting a passenger plane during a disaster are recommended actions that, if followed correctly, can and do save lives. Most passengers find the repeated explanation of these recommendations tiresome but do believe they are effective.

The need for clearly stated, protective actions that empower individuals to reduce their risk seems obvious. During the most intense periods of a crisis, the time for dialog has likely passed. At this point in the crisis, publics want to know what they can immediately do to protect themselves, their loved ones, and their property (Sellnow & Sellnow, 2010). Surprisingly, many crisis messages, even when crises are full blown, fail to include empowering actions. For example, a content analysis of the 2010 *Salmonella* outbreak in shell eggs shipped throughout the United States by two Iowa farms revealed, shockingly, few of the messages provided on network news, including interviews with representatives from the agriculture organizations and agencies, provided clear information to consumers on self-protective actions (Frisby et al., 2014). The story remained near the top of the media's agenda for 2 weeks as eventually 1,300 people contracted *Salmonella* serotype Enteritidis infections after consuming the contaminated eggs. Many of the news stories made reference to the recall and to the growing number of illnesses. Instead of providing empowering actions such as explaining how to determine whether or not eggs consumers had purchased were in the recalled lot, how to return the eggs, or what to do if they had already consumed the eggs, many of the stories simply advised viewers to go to websites where they could obtain this empowering information. Relying on websites for protective information immediately poses a problem for consumers who do not have access to computers or the Internet. Overall, the researchers found that a majority of the messages shared publicly failed to provide protective actions.

In some cases, the protective actions are based on ongoing campaigns familiar to publics. For example, the well-designed campaign to teach publics to "stop, drop, and roll" if their clothing is on fire has saved many lives. The actions promoted in the campaign are simple, memorable, and easily enacted. Other campaigns such as "When thunder roars, go indoors" and "Turn around, don't drown" have helped remind publics to avoid dangerous lightning and avoid driving through flood waters. These memorable phrases enable publics to take protective actions they may have learned months or years before they face a crisis. Equally valuable is the fact these lessons can be shared face to face with others who may not be familiar with them or may not recall them during crisis events.

Some action steps are more difficult to recall. For example, an action statement asking residents to shelter in place may require added information. Sheltering in place during a weather-related crisis may be as simple as going to a basement or to an interior room until the danger has passed. The actions needed to shelter in place are more complicated if the warning is due to a dangerous plume of toxic gas near or over their home, released either intentionally as an act of violence, accidentally from an explosion or hazardous error in an industrial facility, or as the result of a rail car or tanker truck spilling a dangerous substance during transportation. The National Terror Alert Response Center recommends residents at risk of perilous air contamination shelter in place by shutting off all fans and heating and air conditioning systems, closing the fireplace damper, going to an interior room without windows that is on the ground level, using duct tape and plastic sheeting to seal all cracks around the door and vents of the interior room, and listening to a radio or television for future instructions (National Terror Alert Response Center, n.d.). The advice from the center is excellent. Following these steps in detail can and does save lives. The challenge becomes one of self-efficacy. Those at risk might ask questions such as: What if I'm at work and can't turn off the fans and cooling or heating system? What if I live in a lower level apartment? As an extension of the best practice of empowerment, agencies such as the National Terrorism Advisory System (NTAS) and many others seek to address these contingencies. The answers to the questions posed in this section may vary based on each individual's personal setting at the time of the crisis. The goal is to help them understand the threat and to consider, in this case, doing as much as they can to avoid contact with external air. For example, those without plastic or duct tape may block as many openings as they can by using whatever materials are available. The hope is that those who cannot comply fully with the recommendations will remain vigilant rather than considering themselves powerless to protect themselves. Taking as many of the prescribed actions as possible can help reduce risk.

What If Publics Are Given Competing Recommendations for Empowerment?

Communicating a consistent message is a central component of the best practice for empowering publics. Agencies and organizations collaborate to develop, endorse, and consistently communicate best practices. For example, the USGS endorses the strategy to drop, cover, and hold on when shaking from an earthquake begins. This advice is particularly fitting for individuals who are inside modern buildings. Occasionally, however, competing messages are introduced by individuals who see themselves as rivals to the standards professed by scientists, guiding agencies, and other credible organizations. For example, since 1996,

Doug Copp has proclaimed his triangle of life theory as a superior means of surviving an earthquake (Triangle of Life, 2014). Copp, representing himself with the title of rescue chief and disaster manager of the American Rescue Team International, argues those who drop, cover, and hold on are more likely to die when buildings collapse on them. Instead of following this broadly supported recommendation, he explains that, through his years of experience examining collapsed buildings, he has witnessed that those who remain next to an outer wall, either inside or outside the building, have the greatest chance of survival. His theory is that, as buildings collapse, the debris that fall are held up in the shape of a triangle by the outer walls. Naturally, if individuals are in a building that lacks modern adaptations for earthquake stability, the odds of collapse are higher. Exiting such buildings at the onset of earthquake shaking, if possible, is a reasonable action. The odds that the walls will create a safe triangle as a building collapses and that a person can anticipate where that triangle will be, however, are extremely low. Yet, Copp insists the duck and cover technique brings sure death, whereas his technique promises survival. Copp's claims circulated broadly through e-mail chains and social media memes. The theory was even acted out in the 2015 feature film *San Andreas*.

How can agencies and organizations respond to counter messages they believe are dangerous if followed by publics? The earthquake scientific community has responded with a consistent message. Reputable agencies such as the Federal Emergency Management Agency, the Southern California Earthquake Center, and the USGS blatantly reject Copp's theory, arguing that no scientific research, conducted objectively, has shown support for his claims. These agencies monitor social media and generate messages refuting the triangle of life technique via the same channels used to promote it. This example emphasizes the need for attentiveness in both sharing recommendations for action and for countering those competing recommendations that lack merit.

What Is the Role of Empowering Messages Outside the Acute Phase of Crisis?

As we explained previously, some empowering messages are delivered well before a crisis occurs. In crises that arise suddenly, such as fires and earthquakes, having the knowledge to "stop, drop, and roll" or to "drop, cover, and hold on" in one's repertoire is essential. Risk communication campaigns featuring these actions are helpful. For example, firefighters teach young children how to respond to fires at schools throughout the United States (National Fire Protection Association, n.d.). The Great

ShakeOut Earthquake Drills annually remind millions of U.S. citizens to drop, cover, and hold on when an earthquake strikes suddenly (ShakeOut, n.d.). Other campaigns, such as those encouraging publics to have supplies on hand in case of a hurricane or other disaster, are conducted by emergency managers on a continuous basis. The key point is that empowerment can and should be communicated in both times of calm and crisis.

Summary

Empowering messages with specific advice for how publics can reduce their risk of harm can help publics diminish feelings of fatalism and helplessness. For empowering messages to inspire confidence, publics at risk must believe they can complete the recommended actions and that doing so will indeed reduce their risk. The content of these messages is dependent upon the risks at hand; however, they should provide advice for managing the immediate risk as well as long-term activities to enhance personal security. Most important, these messages should be consistent. Competing messages should be monitored and, if they lack credibility, they should be publicly refuted.

Key Takeaways for Communicating Messages of Empowerment

1) The ultimate form of empowerment for publics is to receive information advising them on what actions they can take to protect themselves, their loved ones, and their property.

2) Messages of empowerment are most effective when they have specific characteristics: information that helps the audience understand their personal risk, a distribution of consistent messages through channels that are available to the audiences at risk, a brief explanation of the crisis at hand, and specific, tangible actions publics can take to protect themselves, their loved ones, and their property.

3) To overcome competing messages that are inaccurate or even dangerous, organizations should collaborate with government agencies and other relevant organizations to develop, endorse, and consistently communicate the best recommendations for self-protection.

4) If a risk is well known, empowering messages delivered before the crisis as part of an ongoing campaign can be highly effective when crises suddenly occur. These empowering messages create a sense of muscle memory for publics when they are confronted with relevant crisis events.

References

Arlikatti, S., Lindell, M. K., & Prater, C. S. (2007). Perceived stakeholder role relationships and adoption of seismic hazard adjustments. *International Journal of Mass Emergencies and Disasters, 25*, 218–256.

Bandura, A. (1982). Self-efficacy mechanism in human agency. *American Psychologist, 37*, 122–147 doi:10.1037/0003-066X.37.2.122

Frisby, B. N., Veil, S. R., & Sellnow, T. L. (2014). Instructional messages during health-related crises: Essential content for self-protection. *Health Communication, 4*, 347–354.

Jin, Y., Liu, B. F., & Austin, L. L. (2014). Examining the role of social media in effective crisis management: The effects of crisis origin, information form, and source on publics' crisis responses. *Communication Research, 41*, 74–94.

Mileti, D. S., & Peek, L. (2000). The social psychology of public response to warnings of a nuclear power plant accident. *Journal of Hazardous Materials, 75*, 181–194.

National Fire Protection Association. (n.d.). Know when to stop, drop, and roll. *Learn not to Burn-Level* 1. Retrieved from http://sparkyschoolhouse.org/#learn-section

National Terror Alert Response Center. (n.d.). Shelter in place: Know how, know where. Retrieved from http://www.nationalterroralert.com/shelterinplace

Sellnow, D. D., Lane, D. R., Sellnow, T. L., & Littlefield, R. S. (2017). The IDEA model as a best practice for effective instructional risk communication. *Communication Studies, 68*(5), 552–567.

Sellnow, T. L., & Sellnow, D. D. (2010). The instructional dynamic of risk and crisis communication: Distinguishing instructional messages from dialogue. *The Review of Communication, 10*(2), 111–125.

Sellnow, T. L., & Sellnow, D. D. (2013, July). The role of instructional risk messages in communicating about food safety. *Food Insight*. Retrieved from https://www.foodinsight.org/The_Role_of_Instructional_Risk_Messages_in_Communicating_about_Food_Safety

Sellnow, T. L., Sellnow, D. D., Lane, D. R., & Littlefield, R. S. (2012). The value of instructional communication in crisis situations: Restoring order to chaos. *Risk Analysis, 32*(4), 633–643.

ShakeOut. (n.d.). Retrieved from www.shakeout.org

Strom, S. (2014, July 4). Virus plagues the pork industry, and environmentalists. *The New York Times*. Retrieved from http://www.nytimes.com/2014/07/05/business/PEDv-plagues-the-pork-industry-and-environmentalists.html?_r=0

Triangle of life–earthquake survival tips: Does a "triangle of life" article provide good advice about earthquake safety? (2014, March 31). *Snopes*. Retrieved from http://www.snopes.com/inboxer/household/triangle.asp

Ulmer, R. R., Sellnow, T. L., & Seeger, M. W. (2017). *Effective crisis communication: Moving from crisis to opportunity*. Thousand Oaks, CA: Sage Publications.

Veil, S. R., Sellnow, T. L., & Heald, M. (2011). Memorializing crisis: The Oklahoma National Memorial as renewal discourse. *Journal of Applied Communication Research, 39*(2), 164–183.

Weick, K. E. (1993). The collapse of sensemaking in organizations: The Mann Gulch disaster. *Administrative Science Quarterly, 38*, 628–652.

12

Conclusion

Implementing the Best Practices

As more and more complex risks develop, crises and disasters are occurring more often. Governments, communities, organizations, families, and individuals will face serious risks that could evolve into crises. One very broad risk, for example, is climate change, the shift in global weather patterns associated with high levels of carbon dioxide emissions. This risk will create more extreme weather events, sea level rise and floods, and more infectious disease outbreaks. These events will receive considerable coverage from both new media and legacy media. Effective communication is necessary to avoid crises when possible and manage them when they erupt. In fact, it is just not possible to manage a crisis without communication. New ways of communicating mean we often hear about these crises more quickly. We also receive contradictory information about crises from diverse perspectives regarding what happened, why, and who is to blame.

The 10 best practices for crisis and emergency risk communication we presented in the previous sections are important tools for crisis management. Effective communication can help limit harm to organizations, communities, and individuals. However, they should be used as general standards rather than specific rules about communication methods, channels, and messages. These best practices do not constitute a crisis communication plan but are the principles or processes that should be used to create an effective crisis plan and a crisis response for groups, organizations, and communities. The 10 best practices outlined here also overlap and are interrelated in a number of important areas. In their application, they can work together, complementing and supporting one another. If one best practice is not followed, such as crisis planning, it will be difficult to implement the other best practices. Failure to be open and

Communication in Times of Trouble: Best Practices for Crisis and Emergency Risk Communication, First Edition. Matthew W. Seeger and Timothy L. Sellnow.
© 2019 John Wiley & Sons, Inc. Published 2019 by John Wiley & Sons, Inc.

honest will undermine efforts to build strategic partnerships and be open and accessible to the media. A well-integrated and comprehensive approach to crisis communication is important. Finally, it is important to emphasize that crises and disasters are always uncertain, unpredictable, and chaotic events. Any effort to develop and describe a uniform set of standards must recognize that every crisis is a unique event that will evolve in unexpected ways. This recognition makes communication even more important as a way to deal with the uncertainty and harm that come with a crisis.

Are Crises Really Occurring More Often and Are They Getting Worse?

It is important to consider how often crises happen and how much harm they might create. Are crises and disasters really very rare events or do they happen frequently? If they are rare, then preparing for them may be less important, but if they occur frequently, then preparation is essential. Do crises really create widespread harm? If so, then preparation and planning are important. An essential step in implementing the best practices is convincing organizations they should be concerned about the possibility of a serious crisis because they do happen often and they are very harmful.

Several major past crises have created widespread devastation. We described the 1914 Spanish Influenza Pandemic earlier. This worldwide outbreak of a new strain of the influenza virus may have claimed 50 million lives. The great Chinese flood of 1931 killed more than one million people. In December of 1952, a thick blanket of air pollution settled on London, England. The Great Smog of London was mostly pollution caused by burning coal and the thick haze persisted for 5 days. Some 6,000 deaths were associated with the crisis and 25,000 were sickened. It is tempting to think these kinds of severe crises do not happen anymore because technology and warning systems have improved so much.

There are many reasons to expect that crises are actually occurring with more frequency and that they are creating very significant damage. Powerful risk factors, such as climate change, complex technologies, aging infrastructure, mass migration of people, and new emerging diseases are creating more risks. In 2017, 16 major climate-related crises caused a record $306 billion in damages in the United States. At least 362 people died from these events (Pierre-Louis, 2018). Some of the worst wildfires in modern history and the devastating hurricanes Harvey, Irma, and Maria affected whole regions of the country, shut down businesses, destroyed homes, damaged infrastructure, and took many lives. Although these are so-called "natural disasters" they are associated with the activities and choices of people. Decisions to build communities in low-lying areas, failure to remove dry brush, building codes that do not take into account rising sea levels, infrastructure that has not been maintained, and even the decision not to get recommended vaccinations can make so-called natural disasters much worse.

In addition to crises that are associated with natural factors, many destructive crises are associated with organizations. One of the worst product recalls in history came to light in 2013 involving defective car airbags made by Takata Corporation. As many as 42 million cars were affected in the United States alone. The company, facing $9 billion in losses, filed for bankruptcy in 2017. In 2008, the outbreak of *Salmonella* traced to peanut paste produced by the Peanut Corporation of America, mentioned in the introduction, killed 9 people and sickened at least 714 more in 46 U.S. states. Peanut paste is a component of many other food products, including cookies, cakes, candy, crackers, and even pet food. The resulting recall lasted for months and involved at least 361 companies and 3,913 different products. In 2013–2014, the once-dominant Internet company Yahoo! had a series of data breach incidents that eventually totaled three billion accounts. These breaches occurred at the very time the company was trying to negotiate a sale. The value of the company dropped by several hundred million dollars as a consequence of the data breach. When these kinds of crises occur, they may be so damaging the company never recovers. There are many examples of companies that filed for bankruptcy following a crisis.

The kinds of crises that are probably the most difficult to manage are those that have human and natural causes. These crises often interact, cascade, and expand in ways that were not anticipated to have secondary harms. The secondary harms may go on for years. One dramatic example is the Fukushima Daiichi incident of 2011, which involved an earthquake, a tsunami, an industrial disaster, a radiation leak, and an energy shortage for the entire country of Japan. The Fukushima Daiichi Nuclear Power Plant was built in 1971 and was run by a private company, the Tokyo Electric Power Company (TEPCO). The company had been warned about the challenges of running a nuclear facility in an area that had many earthquakes and tsunamis. The tsunami flooded the generators and made it impossible to cool and control the reactors. The secondary harms from disasters such as these follow one after the other, making the crisis very difficult to manage. Many crises today create these secondary harms because so many of our systems are tightly connected. Electrical, transportation, water, communication, public health, and food systems, among others, are closely connected and interdependent. In fact, the

Department of Homeland Security (DHS) describes 16 critical systems and networks that are so vital that their disruptions could have ripple effects throughout the country (DHS, 2018).

Crises and disasters are often interactive. They cascade and can devastate communities and organizations. They cost lives and they destroy property. Although there are constant efforts to build more resilient communities and organizations, make safer products, reduce disease outbreaks, and limit the frequency and impact of natural disasters, crises still happen. One reason is that the world is more complex and interconnected. The demands on organizations and on shrinking resources are greater than ever before. Infrastructure is aging and is being used in unintended ways. People continue to ignore or discount warnings and risks. These conditions make it more likely that crises will erupt and create high levels of harm. When this happens, organizations have to provide explanations and accounts for what happened and who is to blame. These explanations are part of an effort to repair the organization's image when it has been associated with some wrongdoing.

How Can an Organization Repair Its Damaged Image?

We have emphasized throughout this book that reputational matters should be addressed only after an organization has attended to those publics and communities whose lives have been threatened or affected by the crisis. There are times, however, when the reputation of an organization or agency is inaccurately or unfairly attacked. In these cases, steps can and should be taken to counter the questionable claims. Ample research exists for engaging in such image repair. Benoit (1995) offers an elaborate typology of strategies organizations and agencies can enact to repair their reputations. These strategies include denial, evading responsibility, reducing offensiveness, corrective action, and mortification.

Organizations and agencies can simply deny the claims or shift the blame for the problem to another source. Clearly, if an organization or agency has not committed acts for which it is blamed, denial is in order. In other cases, the crisis may have occurred, but blame for the events should be shifted to another entity.

If organizations and agencies bear some or total responsibility for the crisis, they can evade responsibility by claiming their problematic behavior was the result of having been provoked by others. Another response strategy, defeasibility, accepts that the crisis occurred but offers excuses for why the organization or agency should not be blamed. Organizations can also evade responsibility by insisting that any actions leading up to the crises were completely accidental. Finally, organizations and agencies can evade responsibility by claiming that, in all of their actions leading up to the crisis, their intentions were good.

Organizations can also reduce offensiveness for the crisis once it has occurred. To do so, organizations can bolster their reputations by emphasizing their good works before the crisis. Other options for reducing offensiveness involve minimizing perceptions of damage or differentiating between the current crisis and worse crises that have previously occurred in other organizations and agencies. Organizations can also reduce offensiveness by transcending their discussion to broader, industry-wide issues. Finally, organizations can attack the reputation of those who are blaming them for the crisis or provide compensation to stakeholders who were harmed by the crisis without accepting responsibility.

Corrective action occurs when organizations and agencies make adjustments to their procedures based on lessons learned from the crisis. This process also includes covering the expenses incurred by publics because of the crisis.

Mortification includes a genuine apology for what has occurred. This apology includes a pledge to discontinue whatever actions caused the crisis.

Similarly, Situational Crisis Communication Theory, developed by Coombs (2012), describes four general postures an organization can enact in response to a crisis: denial, diminishment, rebuilding, and bolstering. Denial strategies challenge the connection between the organization or agency and the crisis. Diminishment strategies question the degree to which an organization or agency could have avoided the crisis. Rebuilding strategies are intended to improve the organization or agency's reputation. Finally, bolstering strategies supplement the three strategies described previously by emphasizing the positive qualities of the organization or agency.

Coombs (2012) suggests that some postures work better for certain crisis types. For example, he asserts that diminishment strategies work best for accidental crises, rebuilding strategies are appropriate for accidents or preventable crises, and denial strategies work best in response to rumors or unwarranted challenges. In summary, Benoit's (1995) typology summarizes the strategies available to organizations and agencies, whereas Coombs' (2012) theory is more prescriptive in aligning available strategies with the fitting type of crisis and based on the organization's crisis history. The key point of both theories is that organizations and agencies have considerable options available to them for repairing their images following crises.

Are There Ever Positive Outcomes to a Crisis?

Most often, we think of a crisis as a very negative event and we focus on the harm that occurs. As we have noted, a crisis by definition creates some form of harm. It is also possible, however, for crises to lead to positive outcomes. We have described the kind of optimistic, future-oriented vision of moving beyond harm rather than focusing exclusively on the legal liability or responsibility for the crisis as discourse of renewal (Ulmer, Seeger, & Sellnow, 2007). This approach to crisis communication builds on the learning and change opportunities a crisis creates. Renewal discourse is prospective; it focuses on what can happen next rather than what did happen in the past. It encourages organizations and communities to take responsibility from the very start of the crisis and involve key stakeholder groups in the postcrisis response. Most important, renewal discourse emphasizes rebuilding, rethinking, and restructuring organizational or institutional practices. This may include new approaches, policies, and activities. Renewal can offer an opportunity for an organization to reestablish itself in the aftermath of a crisis (Littlefield, Reierson, Cowden, Stowman, & Long Feather, 2009). Moreover, renewal discourse may allow organizations to fundamentally refocus on its core purpose and values (Seeger, Ulmer, Novak, & Sellnow, 2005).

Ulmer et al. (2007) described four characteristics of renewal. First, postcrisis communication grounded in renewal is provisional and tends to derive from virtues and values, particularly as expressed by a credible leader. By provisional we mean honest, sincere, and spontaneous rather than strategic and planned. Second, renewal is prospective, identifying behaviors and practices for going forward after the crisis that support rebuilding, learning, and growth. Third, renewal discourse focuses on the organization's ability to respond to the crisis and capitalize on opportunities that have come out of the crisis event. This may involve new facilities, equipment, and relationships. Finally, renewal discourse is leader driven and highlights the abilities leaders have to frame values and offer a compelling vision of a postcrisis future that engages publics.

There are many examples of organizations and communities that have used a crisis as an opportunity to create a renewal. For example, following devastating floods in 1998, the city of Grand Forks, N.D., devised a new flood management plan. The plan included removing several houses close to the river and creating a park that can be flooded when the river levels rise without damaging any buildings. The new park helped reduce the impact of future flooding and created an attractive green space for the city. Following the revelation that faulty ignition switches on General Motors (GM) cars had been known to the company for years, GM created programs to ensure defective parts were identified early and that senior managers were alerted to any possible problems. GM chief executive officer (CEO) Mary Barra told employees during a town hall meeting that the company needed to change. "I never want to put this behind us, I want to put this painful experience permanently in our collective memories," said Barra (Muller, 2014). A crisis can create rapid change and allow organizations and communities to take actions that would not be possible in normal times. This may include a fundamentally new understanding of risks and how those risks are managed. In these ways, crises can promote growth and learning.

A crisis can also create important connections between various groups. Communities can come together to help build sandbag levees to hold back flood waters or to clear bush to fight wildfires. In other cases, relief groups organize to provide resources, food, water, clothing, and shelter for those who have been harmed. Customers and suppliers sometimes go out of their way to support organizations that have experienced crises, which may include buying their products. In 2015, the Texas ice cream company Blue Bell Dairy was linked to a *Listeria* outbreak and three deaths. Loyal customers and even politicians rallied for the beloved company and, at one point, 16,000 people gathered for a prayer vigil for the company (Elkind, 2015). As we noted earlier, creating positive preevent relationships is a best practice that can help develop a reservoir of goodwill. Crises can also spur people to work much harder and to have a higher level of commitment to help their organizations. Auto workers took pay cuts during the 1979 near bankruptcy of Chrysler. They also redoubled their efforts to improve efficiency and the quality of their products (Seeger, 1986). The company rebounded and, by the early 1980s, was reporting record sales and profits.

In addition, crises often create conditions where people organize new groups to help reduce the impact of the crisis. Search and rescue teams, sandbagging crews, food distribution groups, and volunteer construction and debris removal crews often develop spontaneously during a crisis. In the case of the water contamination crisis in Flint, Mich., many groups and individuals brought bottled water to the community. In fact, so much water was donated that storing it became a problem. Groups of individuals came together to distribute the water and to check on residents. Social media was an important way for these groups to organize and coordinate their efforts. Some of these emergent crisis organizations continue long after the crisis is over and can create a new capacity for communities to respond to crises. As we discussed previously, forming partnerships with community groups is a very important best practice.

Although we do not suggest that organizations discount the harm crises can cause, we believe that potential positives should not be overlooked. Looking past the crisis to the future, rather than focusing on what happened in the past and who is to blame, can help create positive outcomes. Taking time to learn from and communicate the lessons of the crisis can also be important. We have also found that a leader who is able to help people understand what has happened and suggest ways to move forward can be important in not just surviving a crisis but also helping the organization grow, improve, and renew. Although not all crises will result in renewal, we believe all create opportunities. Focusing on the future and thinking about what can be learned from the crisis are two key steps in helping move past a crisis and toward renewal.

What Are the Challenges to Implementing the Best Practices?

Sometimes organizational culture can interfere with a comprehensive approach to crisis management and communication. Some organizations and even communities, for example, have bureaucratic cultures that make it difficult for groups or departments to share information about risk and work together to develop plans. Many organizational crises, such as the GM corporation ignition switch crisis, are caused in part by failure of one division to communicate with others. It took almost 10 years for the defective GM switches to come to light and the switches were associated with 100 deaths. Some organizations develop cultures of secrecy, making it hard to be open and transparent and almost impossible to develop relationships with strategic partners.

Some organizations and leaders are very uncomfortable thinking about or discussing the possibility of a crisis. Risks are often downplayed and even ignored, which can increase the chances of a crisis occurring. The ExxonMobil Corporation mounted a major public relations campaign to convince the public it was safe to transport oil through Prince William Sound. Part of that campaign involved downplaying the risk of an oil spill and emphasizing that any spills could be easily managed. This may have reduced the level of preparedness. In 1989, the Exxon Valdez tanker spilled over 10 million gallons of crude oil. One of the biggest challenges is that organizations are just too busy to invest the time, energy, and resources to plan for a crisis. Developing a crisis communication plan, conducting exercises and training costs money and may not have an immediate return on the investment.

Crisis awareness usually requires a long-term perspective. Investing in crisis avoidance and upgrading and maintaining response capability are expensive endeavors. Crisis training takes time and is distracting from day-to-day operations. When organizations focus on short-term profits, crisis planning principles, such as those described by these best practices, are overlooked or even ignored. There are many examples of organizations trying to mount a rapid response to a crisis only to discover that necessary equipment has been lost, plans are outdated, and personnel have not been trained.

During a crisis there is also a natural tendency to close ranks and withdraw. This tendency is sometimes described as circling the wagons in response to a crisis and is part of a natural defensive reaction to a threat. Circling the wagons means creating defensive barriers that others cannot get through. Individual managers may feel threatened or fear being blamed and may want to keep a very low profile. In other cases, managers may believe that disclosing any information will increase legal liability. When organizations give in to these tendencies, they lose the ability to listen to stakeholders' concerns, collect information, and respond to the crisis as it develops. Any response becomes reactive and the organization loses the ability to control the message.

Another natural common response to a crisis that makes implementing best practices difficult is a desire to find a scapegoat. Scapegoating involves a strategy of shifting blame for a crisis. Sometimes, blame is placed on an individual employee, a process, or some part of the organization. In other cases, blame is shifted to a stakeholder. Some organizations have blamed customers for creating a crisis by misusing their product. Others blame the media for a crisis. Although it is important to be honest about who or what caused a crisis, scapegoating is rarely a successful strategy. There are always many questions about what causes any particular crisis and organizations should be open and transparent about what happened and why.

Finally, some organizations just do not believe communication is important or that communication has an important role in crisis management. Although we discussed this as part of the best practice of having a process and a strategic approach to communication, it is worth restating that communication needs to be represented at the table as part of the organization's senior management team when important decisions are being made.

How Can the Best Practices Approach to a Crisis Be Used?

The best practices of crisis communication can be used in many different ways. They can help develop a general awareness of risks and crises and the role that communication can play. Managers are often more willing to think about crisis communication after a crisis has occurred either in their company or in the industry. Starting a discussion about planning and response using best practices can be very effective at those times. The best practices can be used to help develop crisis communication plans and can be used as a way to critique and update plans that already exist. The best practices can also be used as a framework for developing crisis communication exercises and drills. In addition, the best practices we described here can become part of the organization's overall strategic plans for communication. Strategic planning for communication usually follows from specific organizational goals and leads to specific tactics. Goals usually include crisis avoidance, resilience, and successful management of any events if they occur. Tactics are the specific methods used to achieve those goals. The best practices can support both goals and tactics that help with crisis communication and with larger public relations functions. The best practices can also help organizational leaders understand that communication is an important strategic management function.

During a crisis, effective communication can emerge as one of the most important ways to limit and contain harm and help organizations learn from a crisis. People who are informed and prepared may demonstrate their value and the importance of communication. Even simple activities such as helping a CEO prepare remarks following a crisis, organizing a press conference, or assembling the crisis team can help show that communication matters and that it is critical to leading in times of trouble. Showing that communication matters is part of the process approach we discussed as the first best practice of crisis communication. When communication is seen as part of the strategic management function of the organization, responses to crises are more effective.

Summary

The best practices of crisis communication and emergency risk communication provide a solid starting point for crisis awareness, planning, risk recognition, and avoidance and for creating an initial response to crisis. Bureaucratic complexities, organizational cultures resistant to transparency with the public, a short-term focus on profits, and the temptation to assign blame to individuals without enacting a fully engaged crisis response are potential barriers to engaging in the best practices. Overcoming these barriers is essential to providing a credible crisis response that enhances safety for all publics involved.

Key Takeaways for Implementing the Best Practices

1) Governments, communities, organizations, families, and individuals are facing more and more risks that could evolve into serious crises. Climate change, population migration, emerging diseases, and technological failures are some of the emerging risk factors that will become more important in the future.

2) All crises involve organizations. Sometimes the organizations are the cause of the crisis and, in these cases, it is necessary to repair a damaged image. This may involve a variety of approaches such as denial, evading responsibility, reducing offensiveness, corrective action, and mortification.

3) Although crises by definition create harm, they can also result in growth and renewal. Crises can create opportunities for abandoning outdated assumptions, processes, operations, and facilities. Following a crisis, renewal discourse can lead to rebuilding, rethinking, and restructuring organizational or institutional practices.

4) Best practices can be helpful tools for managing risks and crises. They are best used as general guidelines rather than specific rules. Every crisis is unique and requires innovative and adaptive approaches.

5) Implementing the best practices requires overcoming natural tendencies to become defensive, close ranks, and blame others during crises. Some organizations believe that communicating during a crisis will only increase legal liability. Overcoming these tendencies usually requires a strong commitment of top management and an understanding of crises.

References

Benoit, W. L. (1995). *Accounts, excuses, and apologies: A theory of image restoration strategies.* Albany, NY: SUNY Press.

Coombs, W. T. (2012). *Ongoing crisis communication: Planning, managing, responding.* Thousand Oaks, CA: Sage.

Department of Homeland Security (DHS). (2018). Critical infrastructure sectors. Retrieved from https://www.dhs.gov/critical-infrastructure-sectors

Elkind, P. (2015, September 25). How ice cream maker Blue Bell blew it. *Fortune.* Retrieved from http://fortune.com/2015/09/25/blue-bell-listeria-recall

Littlefield, R. S., Reierson, J., Cowden, K., Stowman, S., & Long Feather, C. (2009). A case study of the Red Lake, Minnesota school shooting: Intercultural learning in the renewal process. *Communication, Culture & Critique, 2,* 361–383.

Pierre-Louis, K. (2018, January 8). These billion-dollar natural disasters set a U.S. record in 2017. *New York Times*. Retrieved from https://www.nytimes.com/2018/01/08/climate/2017-weather-disasters.html

Muller, J. (2014). Mary Barra's Pearl Harbor moment: "I never want you to forget" how GM failed customers. Forbes. Retrieved from https://www.forbes.com/sites/joannmuller/2014/06/05/mary-barras-pearl-harbor-moment-i-never-want-you-to-forget-how-gm-failed-customers/#416cb5466b2d

Seeger, M. W. (1986). CEO performances Lee Iacocca and the case of Chrysler. *Southern Speech Communication Journal, 52*(1), 52–68.

Seeger, M. W., Ulmer, R. R., Novak, J. M., & Sellnow, T. L. (2005). Post-crisis discourse and organizational change, failure and renewal. *Journal of Organizational Change Management, 18*(1), 78–95.

Ulmer, R. R., Seeger, M. W., & Sellnow, T. L. (2007). Post-crisis communication and renewal: Expanding the parameters of post-crisis discourse. *Public Relations Review, 33*, 130–134.

Index

*Communication in Times of Trouble: Best Practices for Crisis and Emergency Risk
Communication*, First Edition. Matthew W. Seeger and Timothy L. Sellnow.
© 2019 John Wiley & Sons, Inc. Published 2019 by John Wiley & Sons, Inc.